Songs From The Barrio

A Coming Of Age In Modesto, Ca.

Stories and Poems by

Richard Rios

Juarez Chican-izmo Press, Modesto, CA.

ISBN: 1477618791

ISBN 13: 9781477618790

Library of Congress Control Number: 2012910613
CreateSpace Independent Publishing Platform
North Charleston, South Carolina

"If your daily life seems poor, do not blame it; blame yourself, tell yourself that you are not poet enough to call forth its riches; for to the creator there is no poverty and no poor indifferent place. And even if you were in some prison the walls of which let none of sounds of the world come to your senses-would you not then still have your childhood, that precious, kingly possession, that treasure house of memories?"

(RAINER MARIA RILKE, *LETTERS TO A YOUNG POET*)

"The purpose of life is to be defeated by greater and greater things."

(SALVADOR DALI)

"Man is condemned to be free; because once thrown into the world, he is responsible for everything he does."

(JEAN PAUL SARTRE)

"Understanding comes with life ... as a man grows he sees life and death, he is happy and sad, he works, plays and meets people— sometimes it takes a lifetime to acquire because in the end [it] simply means having sympathy for people."

(GABRIEL MÁREZ, IN RODOLFO ANAYA'S, *BLESS ME, ULTIMA*)

"My flowers will not die, my songs will never end; because I, the singer, raise them up; they are scattered and bestowed on earth. And even though they may wither, they will be carried there, to the house of the bird with golden feathers."

(NEZAHUALCÓYOTL, AZTEC POET-KING)

"All paths are the same: they lead nowhere.... [But ask] does the path have a heart? If it does, the path is good; if it doesn't, the path is of no use. Both paths lead nowhere; but one has heart, the other doesn't. One makes for a joyful journey, as long as you are one with it; the other makes you curse your life; one makes you strong, the other weakens you."

(JUAN MATÚS, *THE TEACHINGS OF DON JUAN: A YAQUI WAY OF KNOWLEDGE*, BY CARLOS CASTANEDA.)

Especially for my mother, Guadalupe (Lupe) A. Rios, my father Jacinto Rios, my brothers John, Eddie, and Jesse, my sisters Shirley Corral, and Mary Garcia, and all their families, my loving and long-suffering wife, Graciela (Chela), for Michaelangelo (Miguel), Fernando, Patricia, Jessica, Fernando Jr., Marcos Rios, and Ricardo Campa.

Contents

Acknowledgements

I want to thank all the amazing people who left their homeland and families in Mexico, and immigrated to the United States, legally or illegally, in search of hearth and home in a foreign land, to improve their lives and those of their children. Their spirit of hard work and honesty lent me the courage to make something better of myself.

Thanks to my high school art teachers, Isabelle Barnett and Dale Thorsted, who helped me open the door to a college education. To my college professors: master artist Ralph Borge, for showing me the intense discipline required for being an artist, and Dr. Paul Schmidt, my philosophy instructor and friend, for teaching me to appreciate and respect thought.

Thanks to the hundreds of students I've had the privilege of teaching for over thirty-three years who went on to make something positive of their lives, for allowing me to have been an instrument of change in their lives, as my teachers were for me.

I also want to acknowledge my e-buddy and fellow blogger, William Snyder, for being a fan of my writing and encouraging me to publish my work. *Muchas gracias* also to my loyal *amigos* Carlos Lombraña for his help in editing this book, and photographer Arturo Vera.

Introduction

For many of us today, the term *barrio* connotes a blighted, low-income, crime-ridden part of urban American cities, predominantly inhabited by Latinos, Mexicans, or Hispanics. But about my barrio in South Modesto, in the heart of California's Central Valley, only a small part of this is true. The one-square-city-block was for us, during the 1940's and 1950's, a reserve, an oasis for families of Mexican immigrants who fled Mexico after a tumultuous revolution that ended in 1920. There was no crime to mention, no gangs, only a strong sense of *familia* or family, and community, though we were isolated, even insulated from life within the city limits. The streets were unlit, unpaved, and unmarked. Our street, Flores Avenue, named after the Flores family next door, had no street sign on it.

"Juarez,", as my brother Jesse sarcastically referred to it, was a place where everybody knew everybody's name, greeted each other in passing, and *vecinos* gossiped with their neighbors over wire fences, unlike the six-foot-high ones of today that keep our lives private. They were either related by family, or having baptized one another's children, *compádres*, or godparents. Their kids played together in the streets, and they never locked doors and windows. Though poor by today's standards, I never thought of us as being poor. The barrio was a place of plenty where people huddled together for warmth and survival in an alien culture.

These were rural, uneducated, honest, hard-working people, who wanted only for their kids to have more than they had in Mexico. They clung to their language and culture adamantly, instilling in their children core values: work hard, don't lie, don't steal, study in school, and, foremost, respect your elders; this is what it meant to be called *educádo,* or educated. They watched helplessly as their kids slowly drifted away, forgetting all or part of their culture, victims to assimilation, Americanization.

But there was a middle place between being Mexican and American—call it *Chicano,* or Mexican-American, a concoction, a blending of two cultures—that this book is ultimately about, and its unique contribution to the fabric of what being *American* means. I felt a sense of urgency during its writing. I am not a young man. Only a remnant of the people, places, and things I write of remains. I had to document it now, before it is gone for good, for my family, my friends, for my reader. The *American Barrio* needs to be assigned its rightful place in the history of California and the United States.

To fully understand it, think of place between two extremes: burritos and bologna sandwiches, John Wayne and Cantinflas, Johnny Cash and Cuco Sanchez, Marilyn Monroe and Dolores Del Rio, Pancho Villa and Davey Crockett, Martin Luther King and Benito Juarez, Bob Dylan and Ignacio Lopez Tarzo, Jesus and Quetzalcoatl, hippies and wetbacks, futbol and football, Frank Sinatra and Jorge Negrete, Frankenstein and El Cucui, John Steinbeck and Juan Rulfo, Joaquin Murrieta and Billy the Kid, Jimi Hendrix and Los Tigeres del Norte, Willa Cather and Juana Inez de la Cruz, Plato and Nezahualcóyotl. Do you see what I mean?

I try to look at the barrio, and my own experiences in it, with both humor and pathos. I refuse to shy away from the truth, to exaggerate or underplay it. I want you to laugh and cry with me, just as I did when I lived it and wrote about it.

—Richard Rios

Family Portrait

It's an old, black-and-white studio portrait
with the seven staring stiffly at the camera;
not a smile in the bunch, before an innoculous
hand-painted screen, a forest in a '30s style.

In the back row, standing from left to right
are my two sisters and a brother.
On the far left is John, the oldest, probably seventeen;
the tallest, standing rigidly, a soldier at attention,
Handsome Johnny, ready for inspection.
red-haired and freckled in a stiff suit and tie;
John who never smoked, or cussed, or drank a day in his life,
who always brought me a pair of argyle socks for Christmas, looking
so much like his father, Jacinto; who on Christmas and
Mother's Day, was always the last to leave, always the last to leave;
who called Mom *"Madrecita."*

To his left, in the middle, is Mary, about twelve, dark-skinned,
Indian-featured, and timid, as if afraid, in a neatly buttoned sweater
and collared white blouse; Mary the nurse, who spent
her life in hospitals attending the sick, who put up with the antics of
my crazy brother-in-law, a veteran of the *calles*[1]. How many times
would she help us load him into the car after family gatherings?

To her left, on the far right, is sister Shirley, about fifteen.
Angelic, pale-skinned, red-haired and freckled too;
Kind hearted Shirley who mailed me 10.00 bills
while I played bohemian at college. Shirley, who
shipped me a shoebox full of pork tamales we warmed up
on the steam heater in our barracks one Christmas
when I was a lonely soldier boy stationed in Germany.

In the front row, sitting in chairs, are my mom and dad;
at the far left is the patriarch, my macho father, Jacinto,
his right leg crossed over his left, right hand spread out
atop his thigh, and a white collar folded over his coat;
Jacinto, who drank too much, the life of the party;
who played guitar, and sang like an angel, they said;
he who abused my mother, until she threw him him out;
who bragged to his drunken buddies at Fajardo's Bar
on Seventh Street when I asked him for money, *Este es mi hijo.*[2]

To his left is brother Jesse, about eight, the shortest,
looking scared, his lips pursed, marbles in his cheeks;
his jet black hair slickly combed to the side,
his left arm dangling. Jesse, whose shyness belied his wit,
who relectantly babysat me; who became a tax man for the IRS
who played guitar and gave a fine *segunda*[3] to brother Eddie
as they sang corridos and rancheras on summer nights;
Who recently telephoned to say "Hey brother, just called to wish
you "Merry Christmas, Happy New Year, and *all that shit.*"

To his left is Eddie, the lady's man, about twelve,
so handsome, charming, and debonaire, who
wooed the girls with his guitar and Tony Bennett voice;
Eddie, who loved Cadillacs and fine clothes;
Mom's favorite, though she never admitted
it—the one she *really* made the enchildadas for on Mother's Day.

Last is my mother, Guadalupe, who married at fifteen
and had her first child at sixteen, who knew poverty and the ravages
of the Mexican Revolution intimately, who pressured
my father to leave Mexico to the US so she could better
the lives of her children. Who gave her back to Tillie Lewis
Cannery, a single mother raising the seven of us, and who realized
her life-long prayer to die before any of her children.

They all stare glibly, imprisoned by the lens, expressionless,
unaware of the drama, the triumphs and tragedies that
awaited them in a new country. But conspicuously missing
from the photo am I, still in my mother's womb, the *baby*
of the family, an addendum, an afterthought, the
exclamation point to a story, a saga yet to be written.

Notes:
1. streets
2. this is my son
3. second part harmony

Walking to School Barefoot in the Snow

Not long ago, I visited my old barrio in Modesto. It seemed so much smaller, and I was stunned at how little of it was still standing. Some houses had been leveled, and cyclone fences encircled empty lots. Junkyards had moved in and become parking lots for semis. Doña Margarita's house, my mom's *comadre*, was gone. The Tidewater Southern tracks had been pulled out and the bridge across the Tuolumne River torn down. Flores Avenue, our street, had been blocked off. As I pulled up to our old house, it was still standing, like an old dinosaur. I kept the motor idling as I fought back a swell of tears. I wanted to go up to the front door, introduce myself to the new owners, tell them I once lived here, and ask if I could go inside, but I was afraid. More than thirty years ago, eight of us had lived in this one bedroom *jacál*, or shack, as my mother sarcastically called it. How we did I'll never know, but we did.

As a child, I often heard the elders tell about how tough things were when they were growing up and how easy we had it today. It was the old "When I was a kid, we used to walk to school barefoot in the snow" story. Yet, growing up in this house was, in a way, my own barefoot-in-the-snow story, though it never snowed in Modesto.

According to my older brother Jesse, my dad helped our neighbor and my mom's *compadre* Ventura build our house about 1935. The exposed two-by-four studs in our tiny kitchen were used as shelves. The house had no indoor plumbing and no insulation in the walls. The kitchen, about ten-by-ten square feet, had no sink and no hot water. A single faucet jutted through a hole in the wall. My mom placed a small *tina* (bucket) on top of a wooden stand to catch the wastewater, and when it was full we took turns dumping it in the yard, or to water her plants: *yerba buena* (mint), cilantro, or shrubs. We had an old wood stove that Mom used to cook on. I often chopped and carried armloads of wood from the pile in the backyard into the kitchen for cooking or heating water for bathing.

We had no shower or bathtub, so Mom used two *tinas* for bathing: one large enough to sit in and a smaller one for warm water to rinse with. Our baths were taken on the floor of the kitchen. *"Muchacho cochino,"* she would admonish as she vigorously scrubbed my dirty ears, elbows, and knees with the *estropajo*, a coarse-fiber scrubbing pad. "Ow, Mom, that hurts!" I would protest, but she scrubbed all the harder. The dirty water was also disposed of in the yard.

Our refrigerator was what we used to call an icebox, which my mother kept on the side of the house. The top opened upward and contained the ice. Every few days, the ice man would deliver a large block of ice, carrying it on his back. We used an ice pick to make our ice cubes. Perishables were stored in the compartments on the inside.

We had no indoor bathroom, and this was for me the hardest inconvenience to deal with. Like most families in our barrio, we had an *escusado,* or outhouse, in the yard. It was a single-seater; I say this because some of my friends' families had two-seaters and I could never figure out why. I could not imagine doing my *business* while sitting alongside another person. We used newspapers or old Sears catalogues to wipe ourselves with, but in summer my mother brought us real toilet paper, which she would stuff her purse with from restrooms at the cannery where she worked.

The worst part about the outhouse was, of course, the stench. Sometimes I preferred to *go* in the orchard in front of our house rather than to use the escusado. My fears worsened when my mother told me one day, *"A Doña Luisa, le pico una araña negra en la nalga! Tuvieron que llevarsela al hospital!"* The thought of the poor old woman getting bit on her behind by a black widow as she sat in her outhouse tormented me! From that day on, I never dipped my *behind* completely into the hole, and sat on my haunches, a technique many of my buddies had perfected. The more advanced outhouses had real toilet seats on them. Without saying, those were much more comfortable.

There was no lighting in our backyard, so my mom kept a tin commode under her bed for night use. Lying in bed in the dark, I could hear the scraping sound of someone sliding the pot from under the bed, and I cringed at the sound of a *chorro* (stream) of urine spattering on the floor after one of my older brothers, back from a night of drinking beer with his buddies, would miss the pot! My mother would brutally scold them the next day. Even worse we had to dump the full pot in the morning. We took turns, and I dreaded mine. It was extremely heavy and the smell revolting. I would hold it out from my body as far as I could, but it was about a hundred-foot trek to the outhouse, and you had to walk slowly or risk spilling some on yourself on the way!

But as my brothers and sisters grew older, one by one, each moved out, lessening the congestion in our tiny house. After most of my brothers and sisters had moved out, Jesse and I continued to sleep in a bunk bed in one corner of Mom's bedroom. He and I were the last to leave. Shortly after he married, he contracted my *nino*, or godfather, Panfilo, to build a small room in our backyard, where he lived with his wife for a couple of years before they got their own place. My *nino* was a kindly, ruddy-cheeked man with a built-in smile, who would have made a great Mexican Santa Claus. The room was about eight by twelve feet in size, with no indoor plumbing. When they moved out, I used it as my own bedroom, though it was detached from the house. When my mom asked my brother-in-law, Abe, if there was any way the room could be attached to the main house, he nodded, saying, "*Yo se lo hago cuando quiera, señora*", promising he would do it for her whenever she pleased. In those days, people in the barrio kept stringing rooms to the main house, like a row of boxcars attached to a single train engine, as more and more kids were added to the family.

In time, our house would be "modernized" with a gas stove, hot and cold running water, and a shower and bathroom inside, thanks in large part to Abe. There was nothing Abe couldn't do, and the respect he showed to my mother was something special. How the bedroom was attached to the main house was a feat akin to the Egyptians moving a one-ton block of stone for sixty feet. When the big day came, Abe was the chief barrio engineer.

In the days leading to moving the room, Abe had constructed a track of wooden planks and laid six-inch metal pipes across it, sliding them under the foundation. The room was then jacked up, the cement piers it rested on removed, and the building slowly lowered onto the track atop the pipes. Then, putting sheets of cardboard against the back wall of the room, Abe slowly edged the front bumper of his car against it, and as the car slowly pushed from behind, and the rest of my brothers pulling it with ropes from the front, inch by inch we rolled it toward the house until it connected, all the while Abe chomped vigorously on his dangling cigar! In the months that followed, he dug a hole for a septic tank in the backyard, and then he built a small bathroom with a shower and a laundry room with a hot water heater in it, attaching them to the room. And that was that. We finally had a real flush toilet, and hot and cold running water, and I was king in my new bedroom!

No tiene uno que ser rico, para ser limpio," Mom would say with pride, as she kept her yard spotless, without a single weed. In the summer, she would rake her yard of any leaves or debris with a lightweight rake, making patterns in the dirt, then lightly spray it with a fine mist of water from the hose. The yard looked like a poor man's baseball diamond. Indeed, one did not have to be rich, to be clean. As a kid, I never really thought of us as being poor, though Mom always did. She came from poor people in Mexico, and she never let us forget it.

Sitting in my car outside our old house that day, the only thing I could think of was the line from an old commercial they used to show on TV of a beautiful young woman taking a *drag* from a Virginia Slims cigarette and a dubbed voice saying, "You've come a long way, baby." As I drove off I was immersed with a huge sense of gratitude and sadness. I had indeed, come a long way.

Skippy the Grinning Dog

M y dog Skippy was an ordinary mutt with the exception that when you spoke to him, he grinned. He would peel back his upper lip, exposing his yellowed canines, and his eyes would light up. He was short, tan-colored, and his tail curled up in a reverse C behind him. Once, he attacked my friend Tony when we were mock-wrestling on the lawn, biting him on the back. After that, Tony would sic his dog, Blackie, on him and the two would get into vicious fights. He wasn't the only dog we ever had, but the one I remember most. Skippy slept outside in an old dog house—stuffed with old blankets and with an asphalt-shingled roof—alongside the driveway.

My mom was especially demanding with our dogs, with the exception of her Pekingese. Tiny was allowed to break all the rules and got the royal treatment. Dogs ate leftovers that my mom would fix them: scraps of bread, tortillas, beans, and bones. They were lucky if they got a piece of meat. When the dog refused the food, it would infuriate her: *"Perro maldito, fregado! Vas a ver!!"* She would curse, and put the plate in the refrigerator for the next day. *"Vas a ver. Mañana tendras hambre!"* The next day, she would offer him the cold food again, and the dog usually ate it. But if it refused a second day, she would repeat her admonition, and again put the food away. By the third day, the dog gobbled up the food, even licking the plate clean. *"Te dije, perro maldito"*, she would curse the dog, who bowed its head in defeat.

Skippy was no different. He went with everywhere with me, and on school days he followed me to the bus stop on Ninth Street as we waited for the bus to arrive. "Skippy! Go home! Go! Go home!" I would shout through an open window, as the bus began to pull away, but he would start chasing it, and soon he disappeared as we left him behind.

But when the bus had made a complete circle, having picked up kids on the other side of Ninth Street and returned to cross the bridge over the Tuolumne River toward downtown Modesto, there was Skippy! Having crossed to the opposite side of the highway, he waited for our bus to pass. Over the years we had lost many barrio dogs on this deadly patch of road, since Ninth Street then was also the Highway 99 that carried traffic through the Central Valley, north to Sacramento and south toward Fresno, Bakersfield and Los Angeles.

Seeing him, I would pry open the window and cry out, "Go home, Skippy! Go home!" But Skippy would start to run alongside, totally ignoring my commands to go home as he chased the bus toward the Ninth Street Bridge. He never dared cross, though there was a pedestrian walk on it. Instead, he would veer off and disappear under the bridge and down a dirt path that led to the river's edge. All the kids enjoyed the drama, but for me it was exhausting.

When I arrived home from school, I would take the dirt path behind Abel and Lupe's store, behind the 99 Motel, and across the wooden ramp over the small dirt ditch that ran alongside Flores Avenue, my street. It was about a quarter to three, and Skippy knew it. I could see him standing in front of our house. When he saw me, he would dash toward me, leap into my arms, lick my hands and face, and of course break into his infamous grin.

In the barrio, most dogs never lived to old age. If they weren't run over on the highway, they died of rabies. *"El perro tiene la rabia"* were the dreaded words adults muttered when our dogs began to foam at the mouth and become aggressive, even to their owners, whose responsibility it was to put the animal out of its misery. In those days, no one could afford to have pets *put to sleep* by a veterinarian.

When Skippy got the rabies, my mom handed me our .22caliber pump rifle saying somberly, *"Ten, tienes que matarlo."* I had shot the rifle before, but only at mud hens or tin cans at the river, never to kill anything. I reluctantly took it and found Skippy curled up against a bush at the head of the driveway, foaming at the mouth. As I approached, he snarled at me. He was no longer grinning. I knew I had to shoot him in the head, between the eyes, but as I lifted the rifle and aimed it at Skippy's forehead, I just couldn't pull the trigger! It was as if my index finger was paralyzed, frozen. "Damn it, where the hell are my brothers! Eddie? Jessie? John?" I cursed to myself. It seemed they were never home.

Dropping the barrel, I tucked the .22 under my shoulder, and slowly walked back inside the house. Handing it to my mom, I said, *"No puedo hacerlo Mama, no puedo."* She took the rifle from me, harshly. *"Muchacho verijón!"* she chided. The word stung me. It meant a man who had no balls. *"Vamos a esperar que venga tu hermano Chuy del trabajo."*

When my brother Jesse returned from work late that afternoon, he took the rifle and found Skippy, still in the front yard. I closed my eyes and silently waited in the kitchen, my heart pounding. "What's taking him so long!" I wondered. Then I heard the crack of the rifle shot and Skippy's horrific yelp, which echoed loudly down the dirt streets of the barrio, through the orchard, and down to the river. Skippy, the grinning dog, was no more.

"Por eso no me gusta tener animales," Mom said stoically. The meaning of her words was painfully clear at that moment, and I understood why she always argued against having pets. But these awesome responsibilities fell to *men* in the barrio. *"El hombre trae pantalones,"* but being the one who "wore the pants" was *never* easy for me, not ever. *"Los hombres no lloran,"* was the barrio mantra, but man or not, I cried for my Skippy.

The River

"Let's go down to the river" was an invitation we just couldn't turn down, as kids. We grew up on the Tuolumne River, baptized in its waters. It was our playground, our very own community swimming pool in summer, our Euphrates, our jungle, and our refuge. We could always swim in the pools downtown at Fourth Street Park, or Modesto High School, but nothing compared to swimming in the living waters of the river and feeling the rush of the current swishing around your body and your toes digging into the sand of its bed!

The river was about a city block from "Juarez" and marked the dividing line between the town's city limits and South Modesto, where we lived. The sign announcing "Modesto, Population 10,000", rested just above it on the Ninth Street Bridge. About seventy-five yards across, our haunt was the section of the river nestled in a basin between the Ninth Street Bridge on the east and the Seventh Street Bridge to the west, about the size of two football fields; we easily walked the short distance along the train tracks of the local Tidewater Southern, which began in Turlock and ended up at Empire, a few miles east of Modesto, servicing the canneries and other factories along the way. The train bridge marked the halfway point between the other bridges. And laden with inner tubes, BB guns, slingshots, bathing suits, and the older guys with beer, we spent many joyful summers there. Sometimes we took our .22 pump rifle to shoot at random targets on the water. The sound cracked loudly inside the basin, echoing up and down the river's channel.

On the north side of the river's basin were orchards of walnuts and peaches. During the summer, my mom would send me to pick *verdolagas,* commonly called portulaca or purslane, a sweet, succulent plant that grew plentifully under the walnut trees. She would then cook it up with a little pork, garlic, tomato, and onions, and we would feast on the delicacy. I loved munching on the raw shoots! I would, of course, load up on walnuts and peaches when they were in season.

But our favorite place was an open sandy bank near the falls, just under the bridge. There was a deep hole there perfect for diving and swimming. Swimming underneath the falls was an adventure in itself. You could almost stand up in a hollow space under them and feel the power of the water tumbling over you. "Come on, Richard, don't be such a chicken," my brother Jess taunted as he led me into the deep water, with me shrieking and clinging to the sides of an inner tube for all I was worth. "I got'cha, I got'cha," he would reassure. I learned to swim here. We all did. We knew where the deep and the shallow parts were and often made our way to a sandbar on the opposite bank to lounge in the sun. Nothing could possibly beat the feeling of floating downriver in an inner tube, our legs dangling over its side, our butts in the cool water, on a hot Modesto summer day.

As kids we imagined crocodiles and tigers on the shores, but in truth we found only mud hens, carp, and an occasional egret. One of our greatest thrills was to stand on Tidewater Southern Bridge's catwalk and watch the schools of carp heading downstream to the west. The catwalk, which spanned the river, was about ten feet below the top of the bridge and thirty feet above the water. It was made of wooden planks about two feet wide and could be accessed by wooden ladders on each bank. When the huge schools of salmon migrated upstream to their ancestral birthplaces, the men in the barrio waited on the catwalk and speared them from above with barbed poles tied to long cords. Crowds gathered under and atop the Ninth Street Bridge to watch the obstinate salmon leap the falls on their way upstream. My pals and I sometimes fished from the banks, cutting shoots from the bamboo on shore to make our rods and digging out fresh earthworms from the muddy shores for bait. But all we ever caught were little perches and, if we were lucky, a hefty, charcoal-colored catfish, though the thrill was the same as if we had caught a deep-sea tuna. Few people in the barrio ate carp because of the mass of tiny bones embedded in the meat. I hated fish then anyway, so I tossed any I caught back into the water.

There was a smell to the river, not easy to describe, a smell of damp, soiled clothes; the smell of something ancient. The smell of willow trees permeated the air. The water was a clean, vibrant living organism back then, alive with fresh melt water from the peaks of the Sierra Madre to the east, making its way west through rich farmlands of the Central Valley.

River Road traversed the southern edge of the river and dirt trails darted down its banks toward the water, carved out by previous generations, perhaps all the way back to the Miwoks and the Paiutes of a century ago, and now traveled by us and the tramps that regularly settled along the hollows in lean-tos and cardboard shacks. We steered clear of them, instinctually fearing their deeply gouged, furrowed, and unshaven faces. They smelled of sweat and cheap Tokay wine. Our favorite trail took us down one side of the wooden train bridge, along the fence line of a lone farmhouse built directly on the bank. We never knew who lived there. Near the fence was an old pear tree that produced dark brown fruit, unsightly on the surface, but surprisingly sweet on the inside. It was easy to part the barbed-wire strands, dash to the tree, and stock up on the tasty treats to nibble on at the river. Luckily for us, the farm had no dogs.

One day my brother Jesse decided he was going to build a boat. Like boatmen of old, he and a couple of his buddies, Emilio and Little Joe, spent days constructing the vessel in our backyard. They had successfully done it before. He gathered up some old wooden planks and broke apart old peach boxes, using the boards for the hull, which was about six feet long, and looked a little more like a coffin than a boat... and scraped off chunks of tar that had oozed and dried on the timbers; once home, he melted them over a flame until they softened into a thick smelly paste, which he stuffed into the cracks between the boards of the hull so it wouldn't leak. Oars were fashioned from old two-by-fours and wood slats.

On the day of its inauguration, the three boys lugged the boat to the river, choosing a place of smooth water upstream from the Ninth Street Bridge, near a small tributary called Dry Creek. It was a fine summer day, perfect for the grand event. And with its Chicano skipper at the helm, the vessel floated effortlessly into the depths! At the end of the day, they docked it to a tree in a remote location, next to another one they had built earlier. They would revisit the boats again and again, until one day they returned to find them gone, never knowing if someone had stolen them or simply cut them loose to drift downstream. But you had to hand it to Jesse; it had been an ambitious endeavor, nonetheless.

But as my brothers and friends grew up, we visited the river less and less. And soon the canneries and wineries upstream began to dump waste and sewage into its pristine waters, the fish disappeared, and the once green liquid turned an awful brown color as the river wasted away; today the proud Tuolumne River is but a phantom of its old self. Still, it had played such a vital role in our young lives.

Dicen Que los Hombres No Deben Llorar

They say men are not supposed to cry:
"Los hombres no lloran. Se fajan
Y no se rajan."[1] But I find myself crying,
over anything. Everything.

I cry when you arrive, and I cry
when you leave. I cry when you laugh,
and I cry when you weep; I cry
for the smallest thing: a bird crossing
the sky; a pebble pummeled by time,
the shadow of a tree on my foot.
My cheek against cheek against a cold leaf.

"Why you crying ?" my granddaughter
asks. "Because I'm happy." "Why
do you cry now, Grandpa?" "Because
I'm sad." She is puzzled because
she knows only tears of pain;

Of course, mine are not the easy
tears of women, that flow at the
drop of a *sombrero;* They're hard
tears of machos who labor to
disguise them. But they're real tears,
nonetheless. They count. Can this
be the reason the singer laments:
"La vida no vale nada.

Comienza siempre llorando,
y asi llorando se acaba.[2]

Notes:

1."Men don't cry; they just cinch up their belts and stand" (Mexican proverb)
2."Life is worthless; it begins with tears, and ends with tears" (Mexican song)

Whitey

L iving in the heart of the San Joaquin Valley, we grew up around fruit orchards, and it was nothing for to us to sneak into a field of peaches, figs, apricots, nectarines, or grapes to snatch up a treat during the summers. It was our Garden of Eden. We loved swimming in the canals around Modesto, which were often surrounded by orchards on both sides so, after a dip, we would grab a ripe peach or an apricot to munch on.

In our barrio, most people had fruit trees in the yard, and sometimes we just helped ourselves by leaning over a fence or gleaning branches that draped over it. My uncle Quirino had black grapes in his yard, Doña Margarita next door an arbor of lady fingers. The Morales's had a row of peach trees, and my favorite was one that grew delicious white peaches on it.

We never had to go far, since the orchard in front of my mother's house, about two acres in size, grew a variety of fruits and nuts, including peaches, nectarines, grapes, walnuts and figs. It was loosely protected by strands of barbed wire, but we could easily slide in between them. We knew exactly when each fruit would ripen. I also loved the smell of peaches and stewed tomatoes, in summer, wafting through our open screened doors and windows. Tillie Lewis, called the Flotil Cannery then, lay just across the Tuolumne River.

The rancher lived in a small house situated in the middle of the orchard. We feared getting caught and had many close calls. "Hey! Get the hell out of here, you damned kids!" He would shout and run us off, and we scampered back to the safety of the barrio. I could imagine getting arrested, or shot by the angry rancher. There were a few fig trees on the plot. My mother loved figs, especially the black ones. At their peak, they spit open and the nectar oozed down their sides. Tony, Robert, Charlie, Raul and I would climb into a tree, sit high on the branches, and, like a family of chimpanzees, gorge on ripe figs!

Doña Luisa, our next-door neighbor to the left, had a large apricot tree in her backyard, facing the alley. It gave delicious fruit, but I got to taste it only on the occasions when she conceded to bring a small basket of apricots to my mother. One morning, as my pal Robert and I eyed them from the alley, they seemed to beckon to us.

"They're ready," Robert said.

"Man, they're past ready. Look, some of them are already on the ground!" I chimed in.

The trouble was that Doña Luisa had a fat, ugly, white bulldog who despised everyone, especially me, since I often taunted him through the wire fence that bordered our two houses.

"Come on, Richard," Robert urged. "Why don't you sneak in and get us some? I think Whitey's inside the house." We looked and listened intently for any sign of him, like two Indian scouts, but all was quiet. "Me?" I said to Robert incredulously. "Why don't *you* go?"

"Yeah, come on," he countered. "I'll hold the gate open so if he comes, you can run right out." The wooden gate, covered with chicken wire, could easily be unlatched from the inside.

A quarterback on a third down and inches to go, I weighed the operation. "OK, but *damn it,* make sure the gate is open!" Robert pried open the door, as I stealthily headed for the tree. I proceeded to stuff my pockets with the forbidden fruit, filling my hands with a few more for good measure, but when I turned to head for the gate, I froze in terror as I felt the pain of Whitey's powerful incisors clamp down like a vise around my left calf! The pain, like an electric shock, shot up my leg, and I screamed as Whitey shook me like an angry child with a stuffed doll. Robert slammed the gate and ran for help. Doña Luisa came rushing from her house with a look of horror on her face, calling Whitey off. When his jaws released their grip, I lay helplessly on the ground, my pant leg soaked in blood, apricot juice oozing from my pants pockets and my fists. Everything began to spin and turn white. I don't recall the rest.

Suddenly, a powerful pair of arms scooped me up. Was it God? Had I died? When I saw his pockmarked face, I knew it was Tacho, a friendly old man who lived with his wife across the alley. He lifted me up in his cavernous arms and carried me home. Robert raced home, and I never knew if he told his parents or assumed any complicity in the act.

To this day, Whitey's oval set of choppers, uppers and lowers, are clearly embedded on the inside of my right calf. Each time I see the scar or eat an apricot, I recall that fateful day and I hope Whitey is roasting in hell.

Tacho

He waddled along the back alley like a papa bear
on its hind legs, wading through deep snow, side to side,
his gentle brown face scarred from the smallpox epidemics
in Mexico. A humble, quiet soul, who seldom spoke—
as big and warm as the flannel shirt he wore.

The other day, Tacho died.
That morning, he woke to no sign
of ill health,
And, with his *viejita*[1] at his side,
lumbered into the welfare office
in downtown Modesto.

And while the social worker probed with
invasive questions, indifferently filling out forms,
She turned to find Tacho asleep,
his large bear head leaning on one shoulder.

Noiselessly, like melted snow, he had expired quietly
in a cold, metal, folding chair, so far from
his den in Mexico, there in the welfare office,
while the social worker spoke.

Note:

1. little old lady

A Rite of Passage

During the summers, numerous carnivals visited Modesto. I remember the excitement of seeing the searchlights beaming back and forth high into the night sky. They sometimes came to the north side of town, but more often set up at the old auction yards in South Modesto at the end of Seventh Street. I was not too much for rides with the exception of the bumper cars, which I loved. I was a demonic head-on crasher with the best of them. Once some friends talked me into riding the Hammer, and when it was over, I staggered out and puked. I liked playing the games too but never won anything except for a scrawny goldfish now and then.

It began when my brother Jesse came home one day with a baby chick he had won at a local carnival game. It was stuffed inside a small, cardboard box, the kind they put Chinese food in. Mom hated it when we brought pets home because she knew that despite all our promises of "We'll take care of it, Mom," she would get stuck caring for it. With old two-by-fours and chicken wire, we built a small pen for the chick in our backyard. I enjoyed going out to feed it scraps of food and watch it grow. It was common for people in our barrio to raise chickens and pigs and slaughter them for special occasions, but it never occurred to me that we would ever kill and eat this chicken, especially since my mother had never raised animals for this purpose. It became our pet, so to speak.

But as the chick grew, we noticed it was not a chicken at all; it was a turkey! It sprouted long grayish feathers, a thorny red neck, and big beady eyes. I began to fear going inside the pen to feed it, so I would pry open the gate wide enough to allow me to toss in the food.

One morning, as I was fixing a flat on my bike on the day before Thanksgiving, Mom called me inside. *"Ven, muchacho!"* Handing me an old hatchet, she commanded, *"Quiero que mates al Guajolóte."*

"Me? No, Mom, not me! What about my brother Jess?"

"Esta trabajándo." Jesse was always working. Though I was stunned by her command to kill the turkey, I obeyed. I took the hatchet, and like Abraham about to slay Isaac, I walked out into the backyard and timidly headed for the pen.

I had often seen the men in our barrio slaughter a pig by tying its hind legs to a tree, slitting its throat, and catching the stream of blood into a pail, and recall cringing from its piercing squeal, or being revolted by the sight of blood spurting from a chicken, whose head had just been chopped off with an axe, running wildly through someone's yard! For me, the expression that someone was "running around like a chicken with its head cut off" was not just a simile.

However, while all of this disgusted me, I tried my best to be *un hombre,* as was culturally expected of me. But deep inside, I was a pacifist—a lover, not a killer, except for the birds I had shot with my BB gun or slingshot.

As I stood outside the cage, I prayed for deliverance for both myself and the pitiful bird inside. Suddenly, a giant white cumulus cloud seemed to hover overhead; I waited, but no messages or signs emanated from it. I cursed my brother Jesse for having brought this turkey into my life. Where was he now!

Mustering every bit of courage, with the hatchet dangling from my hand, I slowly opened the gate and stepped inside, not having the slightest idea how I would go about killing this gigantic bird. Should I grab it by the neck, and then try to hack its head off? Should I go for the heart? Maybe I could throw the hatchet at him, like they did in the movies, and hope it would stick into his chest?

The turkey retreated to the far corner of the pen, eyeing me suspiciously, in tune with every movement or sound I made. We readied for war, our gazes locked in desperation, the bird never once taking his eyes off me. Oddly, I had never noticed how big the turkey was. He was as tall as I was and probably weighed as much! And here I was, this skinny, seventy-five-pound little boy about to commit murder on a defenseless animal. Besides, I never really liked eating turkey that much. I wanted to run, to hide but it was too late for that. Whitey, our neighbor's dog, saw me and started to bark. This was it. The moment of my transformation from boyhood to manhood, and there was no escaping it.

Then, in a moment of false bravado, I lifted the axe above my head and lunged at the creature, when it let out the most hair-raising shriek I had ever heard! He spread his enormous wings, leaped into the air, and, claws bared, charged me! Clutching the hatchet, I ran for my life, narrowly slamming the gate behind me!

But just as I stood safely outside the pen, my heart pounding in my chest, white with terror, languishing in defeat, thanking God for my having spared my life, I saw the turkey suddenly stagger, lose its balance, and crash to the ground! I watched in horror at his lifeless body. Had he fainted? Had he suffered a heart attack? Died of fright? I would never know. But sure as hell, the bird was dead. I looked around to see if anyone had witnessed my shame. I had miserably failed my initiation into manhood. I would be the laughing stock of the men in the barrio. But no one had seen. Not even my mom. Whitey had stopped barking. I apologized to the turkey. I looked up, but the cloud overhead had dissipated. "There is a God," I thought.

As I slinked back into the house, I said nonchalantly, "*Ya lo maté*, Mom," having hidden the bloodless hatchet on the porch outside. "*No tienes hambre?*" my mom asked when I passed on the turkey that Thanksgiving Day. "*No, no tengo mucha,*" I said, taking an extra serving of frijoles and tortillas. I have faked manhood ever since.

The Big Red Dog

In order for us to get to the bus stop on school days, we had to walk up the dirt road in front of my mother's house, alongside the dirt irrigation ditch, across a small wooden ramp over it, and continue down a path behind the motel on Ninth Street and a house of an Anglo couple who owned a huge red Irish Setter.

The Red Dog, as we all came to call him, despised us, especially me, because, as I concluded, I had red hair *exactly* the color of his coat. And each day on the way to and from the bus stop, he attacked the wire fence in a rage, threatening to eat us alive if he ever caught us. He would chase us along the fence line until we disappeared, and he seemed to know the exact time we would pass, lying in wait for us.

As we did with most dogs, we taunted him, and his owner would rush out to curse us: "Goddamned kids, leave that dog alone!" We felt safe behind the fence, but it frightened me to think what the Red Dog would do to us if he ever caught us outside the protection of that fence.

One day, on my way to Abel and Lupe's store on the highway, I looked ahead, and there at the end of our street was the Red Dog. How he'd gotten out, I had no idea. When he saw me, he froze, his tail pointing stiffly backward and looking me squarely in the eye, like the bull ready to charge a lone matador in the ring. But I had no sword and no cape with which to protect myself! Sometimes I could feign picking up a rock, and most dogs would dart away. But today was different.

After a couple of seconds, locked in a death stare, the Red Dog suddenly sprang toward me! There wasn't even time for a prayer. I closed my eyes and prepared for the onslaught. In seconds he had covered the distance between us as his paws kicked up a cloud of dust behind him. A stupid thought engulfed me: "Hopefully, somebody will find at least find my bones." From previous encounters like this, I knew not to run from an attacking dog and that the best strategy was to stand still, so I did.

The Red Dog came to a screeching halt directly in front of me, like a baseball player sliding into home plate. When the dust cleared, he cautiously approached, and, sniffing me, began to wag his tail. As I slowly extended my hand toward him, palm down, he began to lick it! "Good boy, nice boy," I muttered stupidly, patting him on the head.

Again, God had spared me from certain death! The Red Dog turned and sauntered away toward his house. Needless to say, from that day on I never taunted him again, and he mysteriously stopped chasing me along the fence. We became new friends, the red-haired boy and the red-haired dog.

The Big X

Our barrio lay between two sets of railroad tracks, the busy Southern Pacific on the west, and the local Tidewater Southern, which dissected it, to the east of our house. The trains fascinated my buddies and me. When we heard the blast from the Southern Pacific trains approaching the barrio, we would run to the end of Hosmer Street to watch them pass, sometimes throwing rocks at them to see who could make it into an open door of a boxcar.

The Southern Pacific that ran north and south was often tugged by as many as four engines, pulling 95 to 120 cars, while the Tidewater Southern, powered by a single engine, carted some 6 to10 cars, not more than fifty feet from our house, snail-pacing its way south toward Ceres, or north across the Tuolumne River into downtown Modesto. The walls of house rattled when it passed. The guys in the barrio would sometimes jump it to hitch a free ride downtown.

During the 1940s, the trains and the river attracted hoboes, tramps, or as we called them in the barrio: *los trampas*. They were desperate-looking white or Negro men, with dirty clothes, unshaved faces, and ragged teeth. We were scared of them. With great astonishment, we watched the hoboes riding the Sothern Pacific trains, sitting on top of the box cars or inside as they stared back and often waved at us. As a kid, I never understood why they rode the rails, why they never settled down, got a job, or lived in homes like the rest of us.

The elders in the barrio talked of *the Depression* of a decade earlier, and how people's lives had been shaken by it. I knew nothing of the Dust Bowl of the 1930s. The tramps built small temporary settlements along the banks of the river: lean-tos or cardboard shacks. Sneaking up on them, we watched as they heated cans of food over wood fires and drank wine from gallon jugs or beer from crumpled brown paper bags. Sometimes, to be mean, we threw clods or rocks at their shacks and took off running.

My mom was petrified of *los Americanos,* as we referred to them. She spoke limited English, so I always had to interpret for her. She was especially mortified when any *Americano* knocked on our front door. Our street, Flores Avenue, was an unpaved, unmarked, dirt road full of potholes and traveled only by those who lived in the barrio. The number *726* was tacked over our front door.

"Andale, muchacho, ahi esta un Americano! Dile que no estoy! Ve a ver que quiere!" And she would hide while I pried open the door to see what the person wanted. They were usually Jehovah's Witnesses; door-to-door salesmen selling vacuum cleaners, encyclopedias, or cleaning products; or social workers. But sometimes they were just *trampas,* begging for food.

For some reason, they always came up the dirt driveway and knocked on the kitchen door, which was on the side of the house, not visible from the street. They were always polite and even bowed when they spoke to you. "Can you give a po' man sumthin' ta eat?" My mother, cowering in the kitchen, would whisper aloud, *"Dile que no tenemos nada!"* "Sorry, we don't have anything to eat," I would translate. "I'll take anything ya got," the man would plead. "Haven't eaten a thing all day."

With no other recourse, my mom would concede, saying, *"Dile que nomas tenemos tacos de tortilla con frijoles!"*

"We only have bean tacos," I would say apologetically to the man.

"That'd be jus' fine," the tramp would respond, and I would tell him to wait, closing and locking the door behind me while Mom hastily prepared the tacos.

As she angrily warmed up the beans and flour tortillas, she would grumble and complain. "Why do they always have to come here? *Van a ver, se van a poner una enchiláda que no la van olvidar!"* Then she conjured up her devilish plan to smother the tacos in hot sauce, hoping that with a good tongue-scorching the tramp wouldn't return.

Now let me get this straight. We *never* referred to anything wrapped in a tortilla as a *burrito* or hot sauce as *salsa.* A burrito, to us, was a small *burro,* and what we now call *salsa* was *chile*. My mom's chile was like molten lava! Come to think of it, she made it by hand in her hollowed-out volcanic *molcajéte*, or grinding stone. To make it as hot as she liked it, she always added some *chile de arbol* (chile from a tree), perhaps the most incendiary of the peppers, which she grew in a clay pot on the kitchen porch outside. It's not easy to explain why Mexicans love their chile, but to eat anything without it was a journey in blandness. I learned to love it as a kid, on beans, on rice, and on eggs. But Mom even put it on her pancakes!

Moreover, by *enchilada* here, I do not mean the tortilla-wrapped kind you are probably familiar with. An enchilada in this case is what happens when you overdose on hot sauce, your mouth and lips are on fire, your nose begins to run, you begin to hiccup, and your only recourse to douse the pain is to gulp water, and that serves to only temporarily stop it. That is a real *enchiláda*.

While the tramp waited patiently outside, Mom would scoop spoonsful of refried beans in each tortilla, load them with chile, roll them up, and wrap them in foil.

Cracking open the door, I would hand the warm tacos to the disheveled man outside. Grateful, he would bow, saying, "Thank ya, thank ya," take the tacos, and make his way down the tracks toward the river. All the while my mom continued her tirade against these "lazy no-goods who ought to get a job like the rest of us. Just wait until he bites into those tacos. He will get the incineration of his life! He won't be back!" She would demonically laugh out loud, obviously proud of herself.

Don't get me wrong, my mother was not uncaring; in fact, she had great compassion for the poor, because as a child in Mexico during the Mexican Revolution, she and my grandmother had often begged for money and food in the streets of her home town, Torreon, Coahuila. "Once," she told me, "when Pancho Villa came in to town and shot up the *hacendados* and store owners, your grandmother and I rummaged through the dead bodies on the streets for money and valuables." Whenever anyone from our barrio went to Mexico, Mom would hand them a fistful of change to give to *los pobres,* the poor beggars on the streets. But this was different. These people were just plain lazy.

Yet the *trampas* continued to come. One day, it dawned on me that maybe the hoboes liked the chile, and that's why they kept coming! They had probably spread the word to other hoboes: "Hey, if you guys want some *good* bean tacos, make sure you hit the green house at 726. The kitchen is in the back. The hot sauce they use is dynamite." I could just see them having gone so far as to mark an X somewhere in the front yard as a marker for the other tramps!

"You know what, Mom?" I said, plying my own kind of wickedness. "The *trampas* probably love your chile so much they've marked an X in the front yard for others to see, and that's why they keep coming back!" She stared at me with that incredulous gaze she got when her mind just couldn't grasp an idea. "*Apoco,*" she mumbled in disbelief.

One morning, I caught her lingering around the hedges that bordered our front yard, as if she was looking for something she had lost. "What're you doing, Mom?" I called to her. "Oh, nothing," she replied, but I *knew* she was looking for the X.

Barrio Brotherhood

As kids, we made all of our toys, with the exception of BB guns and hand-me-down bicycles. We fashioned wooden rifles, swords, toy airplanes, cars and trucks, rubber guns, kites, stilts, bows-'n'-arrows, and slingshots. All we needed was a saw, a hammer, nails, some wire, and a quick trip to the dumpster behind a local lumber yard on Highway 99 provided us with an endless supply of free scrap wood. We had a *season* for everything: a bow-'n'-arrow season, a slingshot season, a sword-fighting season, and a stilt season, until we tired of it and went on to something else. We didn't have battery-operated toys, TV, electronic games, or PlayStations. But we had our imaginations.

We loved to play marbles, with yo-yos and at *los topos* (tops), a favorite. The object was to take turns launching your top into a circle drawn in the dirt, while the guys tried to split yours in half, or at least knocked a chunk out of it with the metal nail at the bottom of theirs. The ultimate humiliation was to have your prize top split in half. Martin, despite his quiet demeanor and skinny frame, was a top-splitting fool.

Another favorite was making slingshots. We scoured the trees for that perfect Y-shaped branch, cutting it to comfortably fit in our palm. The olive trees along the dirt ditch on Flores Avenue were prized. With a kitchen knife, we would strip off the bark, leaving a fresh, white finish on the stem, then notch the tops of the Y, with a half-inch groove. Sometimes we personalized the handle with carved initials or designs, or by wrapping it with tape, cord, or leather.

That was followed by a visit to the mountain of discarded inner tubes in the back of a tire shop on the highway. Experience had taught us that the best, strongest, and most elastic rubber came from *red* inner tubes. But they were scarce among the piles of black ones. With scissors, we would cut half-inch strips, about eighteen inches long each and fix one end of the strips over each tip of the Y and fasten it in place with a tightly stretched rubber band.

We then scoured our closets for old shoes, and cut out the tongue, which was shaped into an elongated oval with two small openings cut on each end. Through these, we threaded the rubber strips, already tied to the Y, and also secured them in place with rubber bands.

The last step was to collect the missiles: rounded stones about the size of a large olive. We filled our front pockets to the brim, or until our pants were in danger of falling off, and headed for the Southern Pacific tracks and the Tuolumne River. On the way, we collected discarded bottles and cans and at some appropriate location, set up the shooting gallery. We backed up to a respectable distance and proceeded to demolish them with a barrage of stones. "Ooh—did you see that? Got another one!" Bottles toppled and exploded, and cans went tumbling. The sound of busted glass and rocks hitting tin cans mesmerized us.

I was a deadeye with a slingshot. A favorite target was a passing train, and, carefully gauging its azimuth and speed, we would try to place a stone through one of the freight car's open doors! Other times, we would punch out porch lights and smash holes in the windows of some of the old warehouses that skirted the barrio. When we felt mean, we shot at cats and dogs, or at the cardboard shacks of hoboes living along the river.

We would stand on top of the railroad trestle of the Tidewater Southern, or on the catwalk below it, while a couple of us would head upstream collecting empty wine and beer bottles and toss them upstream one by one, then race back to join the others. We waited as the floating targets got within range, and onslaught would begin. "Got one! Got another one! Did you see that, man?" We celebrated joyously as a bottle busted and sank to the bottom of the river. Sometimes, we just shot at the schools of carp heading downstream to the west.

One of our most sinister targets was to shoot at birds in the orchard or perched on the telephone wires. "*No andes matando a los pobres pajaritos,*" my mom would plead. But there was an inherent thrill in killing a bird, a living thing. We imagined ourselves ancient hunters, Indians.

One day, as Charlie, Raul (his younger brother), Tony, Robert and I stalked birds in the orchard, we converged under a fig tree after spotting a fated sparrow on a branch. I pulled back my sling, took aim, and launched a stone that hit him squarely in the chest. The poor bird tumbled down from branch to branch and fell at our feet. We looked at each in a moment of awkward silence, and, usually being the ringleader, I spontaneously ordered, "OK, you guys, we're gonna cook this bird and eat it." They were stunned but obeyed. We gathered some dry branches, started a fire, plucked the feathers from the poor creature, and roasted it on the end of a branch over the flames until it appeared well done. Mexicans like their meat well-done.

"OK, now everybody has to eat a piece," I commanded. "I'll go first." I took a quick nibble of the burnt meat. My stomach turned as I bit off a morsel. It tasted horrible. "It needs salt," I muttered. Then, each of the others took his turn. Somehow, in that awful moment, we had melded into one bizarre brotherhood. None of us could believe we had actually done this, and we never spoke of it again. Each time I see a bird now, I feel a surge of guilt, and often apologize to it.

Barrio Justice

Tony and I decided to go to the river, as we had done many times before. We had no real plans for the day, and would probably just skim rocks across the water or sit on the railroad trestle and watch the carp go by. From River Road, a dirt path cut down to the water's edge, where we started throwing rocks to the other side. Tony's landed all the way on the other bank, while mine splashed into the water about three-fourths of the way across.

It was a warm summer day, and not a soul could be seen at the river. A couple of mud hens poked around the brushes on the opposite shore. The sound of cars on the Ninth Street Bridge echoed through the trees. Small, cottony puffballs from the many willow trees floated lazily downstream.

Suddenly we were approached by two oakies, sometimes referred to as "trailer trash", the older one about sixteen and a younger kid about twelve. Without cause, the big oakie started taunting us, singling out Tony, probably because he was bigger than I was. The younger kid said nothing and stood bravely behind his tougher pal.

Unlike me, Tony was not afraid to fight anyone, even his older brother Ramón. Once, we had been picking apricots with his dad in Fruitvale when Tony said something to Ramón that ticked him off. "Take it back," Ramón demanded. "Take it back!" He curled his right hand into a tight fist.

"Make me!" Tony challenged.

"I'm warning you, take it back!"

"Make me!" And with two brutal punches to the face, Tony slumped to the ground. Then, like a boxer who didn't know when to stay down, he stood up again.

"You gonna take it back?"

"No, I won't!" So Ramón knocked him to the ground again. Tony's mouth was bleeding, but he defiantly staggered to his feet.

Thinking his brother had had enough, Ramón turned to walk away, when in a flash, Tony produced a pocket knife and flung it end over end toward his brother. I don't know if he meant to hit Ramón with it, but the knife whizzed past his head and stuck cleanly into the wall of the barn, narrowly missing him! Tony stood there like a fool, when in a fury, his brother came toward him and, with one ferocious blow to the face, leveled him. Tony did not get up this time.

But there was none of that bravado today as Tony backed away from the big oakie. "Come on, leave us alone. We ain't done anything to you," Tony pleaded as the kid began pushing him, prompting him to fight. "What'sa matter, *Mex*; you chicken, ain'tcha? Come on, Mex, let's see how tough you are." My heart was thumping as I envisioned the beating we both were about to get. "Come on, chicken shit. Come on." Tony's fists were clenched, his face beet red, but he did not push back.

When the big oakie had thoroughly humiliated us, he and his little partner wandered off into the tree line along the river. "Don't wanna see you Mex's around here anymore!" he yelled out, and they climbed the ladder to the catwalk, crossing to the opposite side of the river. We stood there, without saying a word, ashamed that neither of us had the courage to stand up to the kid.

But on the way back to the barrio, it hit me. "Come, on let's go get Diego!" Tony's eyes lit up. "Yeah, Diego will take care of that bastard!" He was working on his car. "Hey Diego", I said, "this *pinche* oakie kid tried to beat us up at the river. Let's go get 'em." Diego stood up, wiped grease from his hands on his T-shirt, and said without hesitation, "Let's go get 'em." He was fifteen, not a big kid or even muscular, for that matter, but he could fight. His family had come to Modesto from El Paso, Texas, and rented a small apartment behind Doña Margarita's house. His dad had gotten work at a slaughterhouse on Crows Landing Road. Diego had no love for oakies, no matter how big, mean, or ugly they were.

The three of us made our way back to the river, and I quickly spotted the two boys on a sandbank on the other side. "There they are! That's the bastard that pushed us around!" Tony urged. As if on a mission, we crossed the catwalk to the opposite bank. The two kids had not spotted us. Diego led the way, but as we approached the unsuspecting duo, Tony, infused with a renewed burst of courage, rushed out ahead of us, confronting the big kid. Pushing him on the chest with both hands, he yelled, "Hey, *asshole*, remember us?" The big oakie's young partner began to cry. Tony backed away, and Diego, shorter than the guy, stood before him, showing no signs of anger or aggression, and in a matter-of-fact tone said, "I heard you been picking on my two brothers, huh?"

"Me? Nah, man, I was just messing around with 'em. I'm sorry, man. Honest, I didn't mean nuthin'."

Diego delivered a right cross followed by a left to the face, and the kid went down. "That'll teach you not to mess with my brothers!" Diego warned. The kid slowly staggered up and backed away. "Hey, I'm sorry man, I wasn't gonna hurt 'em. I'm sorry, man." For good measure, Tony stepped in and threw a body blow to the kid's chest. "Yeah, better not mess with us again," he warned.

As the three of us walked away in triumph, I couldn't help but feel bad for the big oakie and his little partner. The victory rang hollow. From the catwalk, I looked down at pitiful pair on the sandbank; they looked so small and helpless, like Tony and I had looked a little earlier; but, at the same time, I felt sorry for myself, for my own cowardice. Still, I grew to admire the courage of these *chingónes* from the barrio like Diego and Ramón, who stood up for us against those who, in the simplest terms, had no love for Mexicans.

The Bigger They Are, the Harder They Fall

I'm probably alive today because I had barrio buddies who stood up for me when I was in danger of getting into a fight. These were guys who weren't afraid to fight anybody, no matter how big or tough the guy was. We stuck together for the sake of survival. Our arch rivals were the oakies. In fact, a little further south of our barrio was the part of South Modesto we called Okie Town, the area surrounding Crows Landing and Hatch Roads.

We often got into it with the oakies who lived in a trailer park across from the barrio. In one of the most dramatic battles, my older brothers and other guys from our barrio squared off against them. As the oakies, about eight of them approached us, our guys formed a defensive line and waited. Meanwhile, as the combatants stuffed their fists with rocks and started throwing them at each other and I watched on in horror, a loud shriek brought a sudden cease-fire, and little Rudy collapsed on the railroad tracks! Our guys ran to his side. An enemy's rock had landed squarely on his forehead, and blood was streaming down his face. The battle had ended in a stalemate, and the oakies retreated to their trailers, but our guys never forgot this, and minor skirmishes would continue as one side or the other dared cross the imaginary demilitarized zone between *us* and *them*.

Living in South Modesto, the school bus would pick us up on 9th Street, after having made a circle further south to pick up more students and bus them downtown to Lincoln School. At one stop it picked up two brothers, Sammy and Vito Montana. Sammy, the oldest, looked like a silverback gorilla; he was fat and weighed about 150 pounds. He was a bully, and most everyone feared him. His little brother, Vito, was about my size,

43

but stockier, and followed in his big brother's footsteps by bullying others, especially me. The minute he stepped on the bus, I could feel myself grow tense. Sometimes he sat behind me and would poke me on the shoulder pretending it wasn't him, just to aggravate me.

For some reason, Vito had singled me out as a target of his poison, and whenever he got the chance he openly taunted me, knowing I was too chicken to fight back. There was an arrogance about him that both angered and frightened me. I would avoid even glancing his way, fearing it might trigger his aggression.

On the playground, Vito would "accidentally" bump into me, daring me to respond. One day during recess, something in me exploded as Vito bumped into me harder than usual. "Oh, I'm *sorry*," he said lamely.

I often wrestled with my friends. Despite my size, I was pretty fast, and when I put a headlock on someone, even if he was bigger than me, I could usually bring him down.

"Say *uncle*! …Uncle? …Uncle? Yeah, yeah, *uncle*!" And I would benevolently release him.

"Damn, Richard, that hurt!"

But I knew it was just play, and if they really wanted to, any of them could beat the crap out of me. Boxing was another thing; I never got the gist of it.

But while Vito stood there, stupidly grinning at me, I slipped an arm lock around his neck and, with all my strength, I squeezed. Then, lifting my feet off the ground, the weight of my measly seventy-five-pound body brought him to his knees. It took him by complete surprise.

"Fight! Fight! Fight!" A crowd of kids encircled us.

"Damn, Richard, I give, I give, I give!" Vito cried in defeat, and I released him. My friends were stunned. "That *hurt*, man. That hurt."

Vito staggered to his feet and backed away, massaging his neck, which was already turning red. Then, to my surprise, Vito stepped toward me and reached out to shake hands. "Shit, Richard, you're pretty damned strong!"

I took his hand. It felt good. I had finally stood up to the bully and prevailed. Vito Montana never bothered me again.

The Faith of a Mother

My mother was not particularly religious in a church-going sense, though she was born Catholic and feverishly devout to the Virgin Mary, the Sacred Heart of Jesus, and a host of saints. She never went to Mass on Sundays, but she did attend an occasional Spanish novena. Mom had constructed a simple altar in her bedroom on top of a mint green chest of drawers. On it was a grouping of religious prints and plaster statues, some of which she had brought from Mexico, and always a votive candle burning in front of them. I loved to watch the glow of the candles dance on the plywood walls of her room and wonder who the object of her prayer was this time.

Our monthly trips to downtown Modesto consisted of cashing of my mom's check at Bank of America on Tenth Street and then a short walk to the Teamster's office on J Street where she would pay her cannery workers union dues. "It's for my funeral, and so each of you can have a little money when I'm gone." Next door was a religious store where she bought votary candles for her altar. Pointing to each candle she would explain, "This one is for your brother who has been drinking too much. This one is for your sister, and that one is for you."

On one prominent place on her altar was a saint who was especially dear to her: *San Martín*, a mulatto saint from South America, holding a broom, a symbol of his servitude, and at his feet a dog, a cat, and a mouse eating out of the same plate. "He was an advocate for the poor", she said, "and many miracles are attributed to him." As a young man, he had served the Dominican order, eventually becoming a Brother.

She was touched by his love for animals and, according to one of her stories Martín served in a church infested with mice. When the vicar announced that he was about to exterminate them, Martín protested, pleading for a stay of execution. He called out the mice: "Look, you guys have become a serious problem in this church, and if you don't leave now, you will all be killed." In short order, the mice vacated the church, and they were all saved. Mom beamed each time she recounted the story to me.

Also occupying a special place on her altar was *Our Lady of San Juan de Los Lagos*. This virgin was pictured wearing a fluffy, blue dress and a golden, jeweled crown and standing on a crescent moon. On one trip we made to the church in Jalisco, I was mesmerized by the floor-to-ceiling collection of *retablos,* miracle boards, hanging on the walls, meticulously painted by amateur artists telling in childlike images and text of the many miracles attributed to her: "Thank you, *Virgencita,* for saving my husband after a tragic bus crash on September 30, 1953, when the bus overturned and he was ejected." The painting depicted a bus on its side, in flames, and the flailing arms and legs of hapless victims trapped inside and trying to escape the hell. "*Gracias, Little Virgin,* for having saved my little girl from a terrible fever." I was moved by the tiny metal *milagritos* (little miracles) attached by the hundreds to the religious statues inside the church, images of people's arms, legs, eyes, ears, or animals, each representing a miracle healing, a prayer answered.

While my mom knelt at the altar, I rambled outside and stopped at a room on the side of the church. Through its open door, I could see it was crammed to the ceiling with discarded wheelchairs, crutches, and arm and leg casts. As we left the church, I showed Mom the room and asked her, "What's all this stuff doing in this room?" She looked at me in disbelief: "Those are the castoffs of people who came to see the virgin and left no longer needing them!"

Next on my mom's altar was *El Santo Nino de Atocha*, a finely drawn lithograph of the Christ child, sitting in a chair in formal garb, holding a basket of bread in one hand and a staff in the other. She had brought this image with her from Mexico. The icon, I found out later, was brought to Mexico from Atocha, Spain, where many miracles are attributed to him. In one, the *Santo Niño* appeared in the thirteenth century to a group of starved men imprisoned by the Moors and brought them food. Through my mom, I discovered that Mexicans adored their *Santo Niño.*

But it was *La Virgen de Guadalupe,* her patron saint and namesake, who took center stage on her altar. My mother had been born on the Virgin's birthday, December 12. She had several prints of Guadalupe, but my favorite depicted Juan Diego kneeling before her in a field surrounded by cactus. A bouquet of roses spilled to the ground from his parted cape, with the Virgin's image imprinted on it. Her robe was made of red, white, and green satin ribbons that had been glued on. Mom prayed daily to her.

Sitting next to Mom on the bed, I listened to her stories about the apparition, stressing to me that the virgin had not appeared to the rich and powerful but to Juan Diego, a *poor Indian.* She seemed especially proud of that. She loved to tell the story, and I loved hearing it. How special it would be for me, years later, to actually climb the steep steps of the hill of *Tepeyác* in Mexico City and enter the chapel in her honor, the exact spot where the *Virgen* was believed to have appeared in 1531, and to stand before the actual *manta* or cape of Juan Diego with the Virgin's image stamped on it, in the basilica below.

Sometimes, on her altar, I would see the statue of Martín standing on his head or facing the wall! "I am mad at him. I'm tired of asking him for your brothers, and he doesn't answer my prayers! He will remain on that way until he answers my prayers!" I often scoffed, saying, "Mom, you don't really believe in all this *stuff,* do you?"

"*Un dia vas aprender a amar a Dios en silencio,*" she would repeat, warning me that the day would come when I would learn to accept God on his terms, in the silence of my own heart.

I often scoffed at her simplistic faith, and she would have died had she known that I was secretly attending a Protestant church with an Anglo girlfriend across town and had actually gotten "saved" one day. I recalled sermons admonishing Catholics to stay away from Protestant beliefs at the risk of burning in hell!

For many years after I married, my wife and I replicated Mom's altar at the various homes we lived in, including many of the statues and prints she used on hers. We often prayed alone or together before it, burning candles for our own children, family, and loved ones. In our current home, it stands abandoned, a faint memory of the faith of a mother.

The Three-Legged Cat

I don't remember the cat's name, so, for the sake of clarity, I will refer to it as Gray Cat. I was about fourteen. Like our dogs, Gray Cat was not allowed in the house. For my mother, all animals belonged outside.

One morning, hearing loud meowing outside our kitchen door, I opened it to find Gray Cat, his right front leg a mass of blood and fur and dangling below the shoulder. I was paralyzed. I lifted him up, brought him the house and my mother rushed to her closet, bringing a bottle of *Aceite del Tigre* (Tiger Balm ointment), and began tearing an old rag into strips. While I held the inconsolable, squirming cat in my lap, she cleaned off the wound, bathed the it in smelly liniment and bandaged it as best she could, fixing the strips tightly in place with safety pins.

We could not imagine what had happened to Gray Cat and concluded that some dog must have caught him and torn off his leg. There was little left beyond the elbow. My mom had me put the cat outside, and it quickly darted off. I didn't sleep well that night, worrying about my poor cat. The next morning I rushed to open the door, but he wasn't there. In the days that followed I continued to look for him, but there was no sign of Gray Cat. I assumed he had gone off to die.

On the fourth day, Gray Cat finally appeared on the porch, but the stench of rotting flesh emanated from the bandaged leg. Evidently, he had tried to tear off the bandage, pulling it so tightly it had cut off the blood circulation. The remaining bandage was soiled and bloodied and dragged along behind him. After my repeated pleas, Mom agreed we should take him to the doctor, so I covered him in an old blanket, and my brother John drove us to the veterinarian's office at the upper end of Ninth Street downtown.

The doctor carefully removed our homemade bandages, studied the wound, and shook his head. "You have two choices," he pronounced.

"I can put him to sleep now, or I can probably save his leg, but we'll have to amputate at the shoulder." I quickly phoned my mom and told her. "Mom, please let the doctor cut off his leg, please?"

"*Y cuanto nos va a costar?*"

"Seventeen dollars."

I could hear her gasp. "*Ay muchacho, es mucho dinero!*" she protested, in a melodramatic sing-song chorus . There was no question about it. That was a lot of money in those days. "*Ay, muchacho.*"

"Please, Mom, please?" I begged in my most compelling voice. After a prolonged silence, she relented. This was unknown in the barrio. Nobody was known to have taken a pet, dog or cat, to a vet. When animals got sick they were put down. It was simple.

After a couple of days we picked up Gray Cat and brought him home. The odor of antiseptics permeated the car. "*Y ahora que vas hacer con ese gato de tres patas?*"

"Don't worry, Mom, he'll be fine with three legs," I assured her. And *fine* he turned out to be. Within a month he was hobbling around the yard, as well as any cat with four legs. The wound quickly healed and soon fur had grown around the incision.

On summer nights, I would lean a ladder on the outside wall of my bedroom, and, tucking Gray Cat under one arm, cart him up to the roof, where I would lay back to gaze at the stars. The Milky Way dominated the night sky, and the stars were exceptionally brilliant, since there were no streetlights in the barrio. Gray Cat would leap at passing flies and moths then cuddle up alongside me and purr. I often spoke to God, "God, if you're up there, please send me a sign"; I wanted something viable, a comet, a voice from Heaven, anything. But there was nothing. I would have settled for a UFO sighting, but there was only my three-legged cat and me, lost in our own private worlds.

In time, I would even spar with Gray Cat, and he countered with imaginary right jabs from the amputated stub on his leg. One day, feeling his oats, he raced down the driveway, around the front of the house, and scrambled up a tree! "Look, Mom, look!" I called for her to see, but she just glanced, shutting the door behind her. While I wondered where his fourth leg had gone, Gray Cat never seemed to miss it, though it nearly cost him his ninth life.

La Lucha

She spoke of it as *La Lucha*, my mother.
A wrestling match of man against the
forces of nature: *La Batalla*: the battle.
War against pain, war against hunger,
a war for sustenance, against stupidity.
La Lucha, a rout with fate; on the
field of battle stands the worthy opponent
with absolutely no respect for you.

The ring is cordoned off with barbed wire;
instead of a canvas floor,
there is cold concrete.
Afraid of the unruly crowd,
the referee just went home,
There are no rules. Every move is a matter of life and death,
a Battle Royál, *mano a mano*[1],
cara a cara,[2] toe to toe.

The crowd is boisterous.
They demand blood! They want their
money's worth. Like Christian martyrs,
we go forth into life's arena,
a vestige of faith clinging:
faith that the lion may die
of a heart attack. Or that rain
will cancel the event.

Now they drag away a loser,
and the lion licks its chops.
The crowd goes insane! They love it!
This is what they came for: *blood.*
Now and then, a winner emerges.
Some boo, and a few applaud.
The victor is carried off
with a branch of laurel
on his forehead. Next time,
he knows, he may be carried
off in a shroud.
For life is a indeed a *lucha,*
A *batalla*—you'd better prepare.

Notes:
1. hand to hand
2. face to face

A Direct Hit

I don't remember how I met Pete, a Filipino contractor who lived in "Tortilla Flat" across the highway, but we grew to be good friends. He had a son a few years younger than me. Ronnie was dark-skinned, overweight, and somewhat of a *sissy*. None of the guys from either barrio wanted to play with him. Pete had a backyard filled with cages of beautiful and prized fighting cocks, and, while I never saw a real cockfight, I knew Filipinos loved them and that it was against the law. And I knew many Mexicans loved *la pelea de gallos*, too. The roosters were vibrantly plumed in iridescent shades of orange, rust, and black feathers, and I would linger at each cage admiring them as they proudly strutted around.

One day, during summer vacation, Pete asked me if I would like to go with him to Lakeport, California, to pick pears. I readily accepted. Picking pears paid extremely well compared to picking peaches or apricots, and I could earn as much as twenty bucks a day! It was early August when we drove to a place called Kelseyville, a few miles from Lakeport. I would later learn the area was the pear capital of California. We left at night, and Ronnie, who came along with us, and I were asleep in the backseat, when we were rudely awakened by the screech of the brakes and a sudden stop!

Pete and another man in front were speaking loudly in Filipino, when suddenly the back door opened and Pete screamed in broken English, "Hol' deez wan! Hol' deez wan!" He handed me a terrified and badly wounded fawn that had probably dashed in front of the car. The deer was bleeding and kicking with incredible force. Ronnie held onto its front legs and I the hind legs with all of our strength until we arrived at the labor camp an hour later. We were exhausted. The next day, they barbecued the animal and ate every part; nothing was wasted. I did not partake.

By Sunday the camp began to fill, and I quickly realized that all of the other workers would be Filipinos. One by one, they drove up in their beautiful, shiny cars: Buicks, Cadillacs, Pontiacs, and Chryslers. These were *nice* cars, not the ones I was used to seeing in our barrio! I was soon to find out how they could afford them.

The camp had dormitories where some fifteen men slept on steel cots, and a kitchen, along with our very own cook who prepared three meals a day for us. The cost of housing and meals would be deducted from our pay. But Filipino food was not even remotely like Mexican food. Much of what they ate I had never seen or tasted, so I played it safe with rice or pork whenever they served it. There was no silverware either, and the men ate with their fingers. I loved eating with my fingers, and to this day I still sneak in a finger pinch of my food, when no one is looking.

The cook, a short, stocky, bald-headed man, looking more Japanese than Filipino, noted my plight and loved to tease me, especially when they served bitter melon! "You no like beeter meh-lon? Ha! Ha! Eat, eat, you like no? Ha-ha!" And he would break into a fit of laughter. In time he took pity of me, and would cook little specialties for me—a pork chop or fried eggs on the side—and we actually grew to be good buddies.

Ronnie and I were the only two kids in camp, so I had no choice but to spend free time with him. Since he was the boss's son, he didn't have to work, and I resented that. He would just hang around under the trees, throwing clods and daydreaming.

The ladders were fourteen feet tall, and to lug one, I had to find its center of gravity and sling it over my shoulder between the middle rungs. It was heavy and clumsy, and I could barely carry it. By day's end you could actually see an indentation on your shoulder where the ladder had dug itself in. Once you got to a your "set" of four trees, you had to position the ladder in a strategic spot where you could pick as much fruit as possible without having to move it. If it was not perfectly set on firm ground, the ladder could topple with you on it! You learned to do this correctly, the hard way. More than once, I was left dangling on a branch, high on a tree after my ladder collapsed under me!

The canvas sack, which held what would be a full box of pears, was slung diagonally across the shoulder. After a day's work, the strap also left you with ridges on your shoulder and sore muscles. Maneuvering a sack full of pears from the top rung to the bottom one was a challenge. Believe me, you didn't want to fall off the ladder with a full sack of fruit, so I learned to fill the sack slowly as I descended each rung, then topped it off with fruit that could be picked standing on the ground.

A full bag must have weighed sixty pounds or more and had to be lugged to a collection point and dumped into empty boxes nearby, where a number identifying you was scribbled in chalk on the box. These were tallied at the end of the day, and we were paid about seventy-five cents a box. The men would began picking at dawn while it was still dark outside, and return to pick after eating dinner until they could no longer see the fruit on the trees!

"No wonder," I told myself, "they drive these new, shiny cars."

It was a warm Sunday afternoon when the small van pulled in to the camp unannounced. The men looked at one another and grinned. We heard giggles and saw four or five young girls with heavy makeup exit. One of the men led them into the latrine. Ronnie and I looked on in dismay.

"What'er they doing?" he asked stupidly.

"Beats me," I said, shrugging my shoulders. One by one, the men entered the room, exiting some time later with a slight grin on their faces.

"Let's go see what's going on," I urged Ronnie. Undetected, we made our way to the back of the latrine and found a knothole to peer through. Ronnie was first. "Look, look, it's the cook! What's he doing?" Ronnie whispered to me.

"Let me look", I said, shoving him aside. Realizing that Ronnie had no idea what was going on, I said, "He's doing pushups!" Though the small hole, the only thing visible was the cook going up and down, sweating profusely and his eyes shut tightly; I could hear him groaning. I never told anyone about this.

The next day, daydreaming at the top of the ladder, I saw Ronnie standing idly by, about one row of trees over. The thought of him just loafing and still getting paid by his dad infuriated me. As if possessed, I descended my ladder slowly and searched the ground for a mushy, half-rotten pear. Finding it, I rotated it until if fit perfectly in my palm. I visualized the distance, the angle, and the height needed to hit my target, and launched the pear as hard as I could into the sky.

I held my breath as I watched the pear reach its arc, and descend in the direction of Ronnie. It splattered squarely on his forehead. Like a dog that had just been kicked, Ronnie squealed and began to cry. I scurried to the top of my ladder and continued picking. As I bit into a juicy, ripe pear on the top rung, I savored my victory. I don't think Ronnie ever knew who had thrown that pear. It had been a direct hit.

Life from the Back of a Truck

"Estúdia. No seas burro. Prepárate para un trabájo bueno donde estés el la sombra y no andes en el sol como animál."

Louie Garcia, my best friend's dad, was a great guy. He was a dark-skinned, short, stocky man, looking more Asian than Mexican. In fact, I was quite familiar with the odd Mexican terms *Mi Chinito, Mi Chinita,* referring to the Chinese features present in many Mexicans. Robert, his son, was a few months older than me, and we regularly ran around together, riding our bikes, shooting BB guns, and playing war and cowboys-and-Indians. His mom, Doña Cuca, was always nice to me, often inviting me to dinner at their house. I loved her rice and *frijoles con queso,* beans with cheese. But what struck me as strange was that all the men would sit down to eat first, while the women brought them *seconds* and freshly warmed tortillas. When they were done eating and left the table, the women would sit to eat.

This would never happen at my house. My mom cooked the food, left it on the stove, and, as each of us arrived, he or she would serve him- or herself. Few were the times when we sat down to eat as a family. This seemed normal to me. Mom was practical that way, though she and I would often eat together, after all my brothers and sisters had married and left home. I was the last to go.

Louie was a labor contractor. He owned a large truck, the back covered with a canvas tarp. He had built wooden benches on each side of the bed, able to seat about a dozen workers. During the summers I loved going with Robert and Louie to pick fruit in the fields. We harvested apricots, peaches, and grapes. The workers were men who lived in the barrio and a few *mojados* or wetbacks, as we sometimes called them.

I would arise at 5:00 a.m. My mother was already up fixing my breakfast of *huevos con frijoles*, beans with eggs, which tasted extra good at that time of day. As I ate, she prepared my *lonche*, tacos with scrambled eggs and beans, sometimes eggs with chorizo, sometimes with only beans. We hardly ever ate sandwiches. She put the tacos in a brown paper bag. And I was off, walking across our backyard into the alley, down a couple of houses, and through a gate to Robert's house. It was still dark outside.

We would pile into the back of Louie's truck, and I joined in the lively chatter of the men: *"Buenos días."*

"Vamonós al jale!" *Jale* was a slang term for the Spanish verb *jalar*, to pull, referring to the pulling of fruit from branches. Robert and I were the only two kids among the workers. But of course, he rode up front with his dad. I enjoyed being with the *men. "Hola, güerito", como estas?"* They loved to make fun of my light complexion.

We drove down Hosmer Street and right onto the old Highway 99, heading for Ceres, this time, to an apricot orchard owned by an old, friendly, Italian rancher.

As we unloaded, the fields were still dark, and we could see only silhouettes. This was the best part of day. It was damp and cool, and droplets of dew still clung to the leaves. Faint beams of sunlight could be seen lighting the crests of the Central Range to the west. The men wasted no time. *"A piscar! A piscar!"* would echo through the trees as Louie commanded us to start picking. We wasted no time, knowing it would be a hot one today, ninety-nine degrees by one o'clock. And the men wanted to pick as much as they could while it was still cool.

They rushed to grab a ladder and a bucket and choose a fresh set of four trees, scampering up the ladders to begin picking; you could hear the "plunk, plunk, plunk" of the fruit hitting the bottoms of the tin buckets. In the dim light of early dawn, the fruit on the branches was barely visible. The men jabbered in Spanish from tree to tree and sang Mexican songs, and I fantasized about how dapper I would look walking down the hallways at school in the fall, in my sporty, blue-suede shoes, khaki pants, and cashmere sweaters I would buy with the money I earned. Of course, Robert, being the contractor's son, did not have to pick. He "swamped," or stacked full boxes on the backs of trucks, or checked the fruit for proper size with a little plastic ring.

The time passed quickly and soon it was ten o'clock; daydreaming and nibbling on a ripe apricot, I would linger at the top of the ladder. Apricots were easy to pick. I hated the peaches. They had fuzz, a fine powder that spilled into the air in a little dust cloud and irritated my eyes and nose. Worse, it collected around the collar of my shirt and stuck to the sweat and crud, causing my neck to itch. I couldn't wait to get home to shower it off.

While I was a lazy worker—I had no sense of urgency—I was steady. Five or ten dollars for a day's work was good enough for me. That was big money in those days, when hamburgers were four for a buck, and gas twenty-five cents a gallon. Conversely, the men who depended on the wages to support their families worked hard, but they were no match for the *mojados* who stripped the branches and trees like mad locusts; these men needed to earn as much money as they could to send to their families in Mexico. Unlike many of my friends whose entire earnings were taken from them to help support the family, I kept mine; my mom never took a dime from my check. "What you make is yours," she said.

But my favorite time of the day was noon, and lunch! *"Vámonos a comer! Vámonos a comer!"* Louie's voice invited us to lunch. By eleven o'clock, Louie had already started a bonfire with dried branches from the trees. We left our ladders and congregated near the fire in a large circle. Grabbing a forked tree branch, we secured a *taco* on it, holding it over the fire to warm it up. Let me tell you, there was nothing better than sitting on a mound of clods, under a fruit tree in the shade, in the middle of an orchard with hardworking *men,* and eating warmed bean tacos! The rancher brought a gallon of red wine, and I would sneak a couple of swigs with the workers. It made me giddy.

Having only thirty minutes for lunch, we chewed and swallowed fast, so we could have ten or fifteen minutes left over for a quick snooze. I would quickly curl up into a fetal position and fall into a deep sleep. But not for long. *"Vamo-nós a trabajar! Vamo-nós a trabajar!"* Louie's voice sang out rhythmically, purposely elongating the words; our moment of rest was over, and it was back to *el jale*.

By one o'clock it was unbearable, and already close to a hundred degrees. Work slowed. It was hot even in the shade! Mercifully, by two o'clock Louie's voice rang out again, this time bringing the good news: *"Vámonos a la casa! Vámonos a la casa!"* And the men slowly slipped down the ladder, each filling one last bucket with fruit, and headed for the truck.

On the way back, the mood had changed. The men were silent, exhausted, dirty, and sweaty. The trip home seemed much longer. The smell of sweat and grime filled the truck. Workers drifted off, their bodies gently swaying back and forth with the bumps of the highway. I was elated to see the truck turn onto Hosmer Street, over the train tracks and pull up to Robert's house; the men spilled out and went their ways. *"Hasta mañana!"* Louie called. *"Oh, my God, not again tomorrow,"* I thought.

I trudged into the house, stripped off my dirty clothes, and headed straight for the shower. The cold water felt delicious as I watched the dirt and grime slip down my arms and legs, swirl between my toes, and rush down the drain.

As I plunked down on my bed, my entire body hurt. My shins ached from the rungs of the ladder; my hands and back, from the day's picking and carrying full buckets of fruit to be tallied. "Mom is right," I thought to myself. I would have to study hard in school and prepare myself for a job in the shade, something in an air-conditioned office. This was indeed a job for *burros*. Yet I worried for the young men in the back of Louie's truck who didn't have the choice to go to school. They toiled to help support their families. It just wasn't fair.

"Como te fue?" my mom would call out. "It went fine, Mom." Drifting off to sleep at night, after a hard day's work, I felt good inside. I had *earned* my pay. I had worked and sweated with *men*. And I would sleep like a *man*.

The Mojado

Agapito, the ruddy, old, cantankerous Mexican *mojado*
on the porch of my mother's *comadre*'s
backyard shack, sang Mexican songs
to the summer nights.

"What's a *mojado*?" I asked my mother.
"It's what they call people who swim the Rio Grande;
vienen a trabajar para mantener sus familias.[1]
They go back to Mexico in the winter."

"Where's Agapito, Mom?"
"Anoche se lo llevo la Migra, pobrecito."[2]
"Where did they take him?"
*"A Mexico. Pobrecito, nadamas para
tener que volverse a cruzar."*[3]

And a week later Agapito was back
on that porch again, singing Mexican songs.
And I wondered what all the fuss was about
these illegal aliens.

In the orchards shrewd bronze hands stripped
peaches and apricots from branches
like Future Farmers of America in a milking contest,
pulling teats this way and that.

Like athletes in Olympic competition, masterful hands
worked to see who could pick the most boxes and
and send the biggest check to their families that week.
Men fifty to sixty years old, boys sixteen or seventeen,
entire families worked.

Like voracious locusts in a virgin cornfield,
they stripped orchards under a vengeful sun
and dreamed of mercados and plazas; of what
dólares will buy in Mexico when they returned.

Then dreams shattered with the dreaded cry:
"Ahi viene La Migra!"[4] And they scattered like
cucarachas[5] from under overturned stones,
running for their very lives.

And they ran, sometimes into cyclone fences,
barbed wire, sometimes into rivers or canals
that claimed their souls;
and tears would fall a thousand miles away.

But the *mojados* would be back in a few days
to pick again, never having claimed their rightful pay.
"Anoche se llevaron a Agapito otra vez,"[6]
I would hear for many summers to come.

Notes:

1. "They come to work in order to support their families in Mexico"
2. "Last night the immigration officers took him, poor man"
3. "Poor people, they take them back, only for them to turn around and return"
4. "Here come the immigration officers!"
5. cockroaches
6. "Last night they took Agapito again"

Three Fingers of Flour and Two of Salt

"My mother was the best cook in the world", is something most of us say about our mothers' cooking. My mom never cooked up any fancy dishes for us, and her recipes were all handed down from her mother and her mother's mother, before her, *never* written down. The staples were beans and tortillas, with special dishes on Mother's Day and Christmas, when the whole clan got together. She cooked her *frijoles* in a simple clay pot from Mexico, putting a small plate on top for creating steam. The pot, burned black on its bottom, was lopsided. We would feast on *frijoles del oya,* or boiled beans, topped with cilantro and hot salsa, and served with her freshly made flour tortillas.

Sometimes, for a special treat, we would buy a loaf of French bread from a bakery on Tenth Street to eat the beans with. She loved to cut off the elbows of the loaf and dip them into the beans. A couple of days later, she would make the leftover beans into *refritos.* Even from the next room, I could hear the hiss of the beans as she scooped them into the hot *manteca* or lard, "Zzzzzzzzzt!" Under a low flame, she then let them simmer until they thickened into a paste. "*El sabor está en la mantéca.*" And indeed, the lard was where their great taste lay. I could never decide if I liked *frijoles del oya* or *refritos* best. I could eat beans every day of my life and never tire of them.

In those days, corn tortillas were unheard of; you couldn't even buy them in the stores, so she made flour tortillas every few days. "*Ay, muchacho mira que feas me salieron,*" she would fret when they turned out lopsided. "I don't care, Mom, they taste just as good," I would assure her. She used a specially made heavy, round, cast iron grill she had saved from her old wood stove for cooking each tortilla, and in swift sure movements flipped each over without ever burning her fingers. To this day, I can never warm up tortillas over an open flame, like she so often did, without burning my fingers!

Like clockwork, she was up every day at 5:00 a.m. whether she was working or not. Half asleep, I could hear the "click-clack, click-clack, click-clack" of the *palóte* (rolling pin) as it rolled off the edge of the tortilla dough onto the wooden kneading board. I loved to watch them *inflarse,* or puff up like little flat balloons on the stove. Our special treat as kids was to take a freshly made tortilla, put butter in inside, roll it up, and eat it. She would store them in bowl, wrapped in a towel, and they would stay fresh and soft for days. When they got hard, she would grill the tortillas on each side over an open flame until they actually charred. Then she would break them into pieces and use them to scoop up the *refritos.*

Her cuisine was simple, and *papas* (potatoes) *con wienies*, was one of my favorites. *"Comida de los pobres", food of the poor*, she would quip. But to me, fried potatoes with wieners were delicious. She also made delicious *cocido* (soup), *albondigas* (rice meatballs), and *picadillo* (a hamburger and potato stew). On Christmas and Mother's Day it was different. It would not be Christmas without tamales, or Mother's Day without enchiladas.

She made everything from scratch. For the making of tamales, we started the day before, and my job was to grind the dried, large, red chiles and corn that had been soaked and softened overnight in buckets of water in our *molino* fastened to a post outside. The ground corn became thick masa, or cornmeal, which would later be softened with hot lard and salted. The chilies became a blood red sauce that would be sifted to get rid of the skins, and later simmered and seasoned into a rich paste.

Next, there was the rinsing of the corn husks, and we all pitched in to *embarrar la masa*, or to spread the corn meal onto the leaves with the backsides of spoons. During the tedious ritual, we joked and gossiped, and there was a great feeling of family and community. But the secret to the unique taste of Mom's tamales lay in the *comino,* or cumin, that was added in the chile sauce, which was laden with chunks of pork. With the trimmed fat from the pork she made *chicharrones,* or pork rinds, and we all scrambled to make sure we got some before the tamales were cooked! Filling a freshly cooked flour tortilla with the *chicharrones* was a heavenly delight. After the leaves were spread with masa, a spoonful of the chili sauce was placed inside, and the final touch was to set a black, unpitted olive into the sauce because, as Mom put it, "the pitted ones don't have the flavor." Each *tamal* was neatly stacked in a large pot for cooking.

For Mother's Day it was enchiladas made with flour tortillas instead of the traditional corn tortillas. Again, she made fresh sauce from red chiles to fry the tortillas in, but hers had no meat in them, only shredded lettuce, diced onions, and black olives. Once fried, she would stuff each one with shredded lettuce and grated onions and top them with grated, hard, dry, Jack cheese (only one store in Modesto sold it), and roll them into cylinders. Afterward, they were placed in the oven to gently toast them. We loved eating the leftover enchiladas with fried eggs and refried beans the next day!

If this was *comida de los pobres,* I wondered how rich people ate!

But there were some dishes Mom cooked that I had to pass on. One was fried cow's brains, or *cezos*! Thanks, but no thanks. Another was *tripas,* or fried intestines! The stink filled the kitchen and wafted outside if the windows were open. I also had a little trouble with *lengua*, or beef tongue. Just the sight of a giant pale tongue in the package made me a little ill. *Moronga*, or blood sausage, was another of her delights I avoided. Ultimately I was a beans-and-tortillas man.

Menudo was another thing, if you could get past the awful smell of cooked tripe. We would open the doors and windows, and I always found excuses for going out during the process. I actually loved menudo, especially how Mom loaded the soup with hominy. She always made a point of cutting the stomach lining into small pieces, in contrast to the way others prepared it. I hated the "y-yank, y-yank, y-yank" of my molars trying to tear through huge pieces of the meat. Often, I found strange things floating around in my bowl, so I would respectfully and cautiously push them to the side. A squirt of lime, a dash of chopped cilantro and onions, and a spoonful of chile was all that was needed to complete the dish.

The few times I invited my gringo friends over to eat, she was tormented with embarrassment. "*Para que los invitastes? Ya sabes que no tememos nada que ofrecerles; nomas frijoles y tortillas!*" But beans and tortillas was all it took for them to hound me: "Hey Richard, when you gonna invite us to your mom's place to eat again?"

My wife still preserves many of my mom's recipes, which she too has never written down. It remains *tres dedos de harina* or *dos dedos de sal* as she holds up three fingers for how much flour, or two fingers for the precise measurement of salt needed for a dish.

Dracula, Frankenstein, Wolf Man, El Cucui, El Diablo, and La Llorona

---

Embedded deep in my psyche as a young boy were the awful visages of demons, ghosts, monsters, and bogeymen, especially those in Hollywood movies. Nothing was scarier than when my friends and I would watch the Wolf Man begging to be locked in a room on the eve of a full moon. "No matter what I do or say, don't open the door!" His tormented howl sent chills up our spines as he began to sprout fangs and tufts of hair on his hands and face. There was also Count Dracula rising from his coffin and sinking his incisors into the white throat of a screaming damsel. We shrank with him when a silver crucifix was thrust into his face, a victory of good over evil, and the wooden stake was mercilessly pounded into his chest at the end of the movie.

Then there was Frankenstein, sewn together from parts of dead corpses, his rigid body stumbling forward, arms extended, ready to lock someone in his powerful death grip. In the dark movie houses, we howled and stamped our feet while the girls cupped their hands over their eyes and screamed; but we loved it, and we ate it up with heaps of popcorn.

But the barrio had its own set of bogeymen. My mother was a master at telling stories from the old country; all, she claimed, were true, because people said it had actually happened to them or someone they knew. We grew up on stories about the *Cucui* (coo-cooey), a monster that ate little kids who stayed out late at night. *"No andes afuera cuando obscuresca,"* she would warn, *"sino se los va agarrar el Cucui!"* Late at night, lying in my bed, I swear I could hear *El Cucui* outside our house, his footsteps crunching on the gravel of the nearby train tracks. "Listen, it's the *Cucui*!" I would tell my frightened nephew, Miguel, and we would hide under the covers.

We got a generous dose of *El Diablo,* the Devil, and our greatest fear was to meet him face to face on a dark night. My mom had several stories of this happening to someone in Mexico. One story I most remember concerns a young girl who went to a dance against her mother's wishes. "Be home at midnight," her mother warned, "because terrible things can happen to a young girl without an escort." Undaunted, at the dance she quickly caught the eye of the most handsome young man on the floor. She was smitten.

When he asked her to dance, she fell into his arms. The most coveted girl at the dance, she gloried in the adulation of the other girls as she danced song after song with him. But before she realized it, the clock had stuck the midnight hour! When the music stopped, and the lights came on, something caused her look down at her partner's shoes, and there she saw the *hooves* of a goat! She had danced with the devil! I get a chill now just telling you this story.

Of course, it didn't help matters that I, too, often disobeyed my mother. "*Te va agarrar El Diablo por maldito y mentiroso,*" my mother would warn. After each lie, evil deed, and nasty thought, I was certain *El Diablo* would snatch me up. "*Ten cuidado,*" Mom would admonish me, "*No sea que el diablo ande agatas!*" I just could picture Satan sneaking around on his knees and waiting for his chance to pounce on me. "We all have a little angel on one shoulder, telling us to do good, and a little devil on the other prompting us to evil," Mom would explain. Sometimes, I believed God had skipped the angel, giving me a devil on each shoulder instead! *El Diablo* was red, had horns on his head, the feet of a goat, a long, pointed tail, and a pitchfork with which to torment his victims within the eternal flames of Hell!

But my favorite was the story of *La Llorona* (The Weeping Lady). Though I have heard other variations since, I loved my mother's version best. It concerned a poor woman in Mexico who was married to a cruel man who drank and beat her. He was a womanizer who flaunted his infidelity, greatly tormenting her. In a moment of desperation, and to avenge her husband's public humiliation of her, she took her five children to the river and drowned them one by one. When she died sometime later, she found herself face to face with God, who asked, "Where are your children?" "I have l-lost them", she stammered. "Where did you lose them?" God persisted.

"In the river."

"Woman, I know you have drowned your children in the river. I want you to return to earth, and when you find them, bring all of them to me."

"But, I have no idea where they have gone!" She protested. "The river's current has taken them away!"

According to my mother, "The poor woman returned to earth and began searching the river for the corpses of her children, but she never found them, and to this day, near any river, lake, or waterway, at dusk, if you listen closely, you will hear her cry in the wind, *"Aaaaay, mis hijos; aaaaay, mis hijos."* I can swear to you myself that my friends and I heard *La Llorona* more than once at the Tuolumne River. "Did you hear that?"

"Hear what?"

"Shut up, *pendejo*! Listen!" Then one of us would shout, "Oh shit, it's *La Llorona!*" And Robert, Tony, Charley, Raul, and I would race home in the dark. If you don't believe all this stuff, go ahead; go to a river or lake at dark alone. I dare you.

Tragically, the innocence of these childhood encounters with evil and the supernatural ended the day we stepped into the theater to watch Alfred Hitchcock's *Psycho*. It would be a new ball game now, and the terror might lie in the kid next door.

The Weeping Woman

Aaaaaiiiieee, mis hijos—
Aaaaaiiiieee, mis hijos.[1]

They say she wails at dusk
into the black marshes, creeks, rivers,
and lakes of the Americas. For in a fit
of rage she drowned her babies
at the river, one by one,
when she discovered her man
had been unfaithful to her;
and the river's currents
se los llevo a la chingada[2]
so that now she can't find them!

And the story goes that when
she died and went to heaven,
God would not let her in!
"Where are your children?"

"I don't know. The river took them!"

"Woman, you go back to earth;
find them and bring them to me."

Now *la pobrecita*[3] traverses
the earth's waterways at dusk; calling out
to them. Sometimes the wind
echoes her wail and if you

listen closely, you will hear
her lament: it is the travail of a mother
giving birth to pain,
giving birth to torment.
Should I run or should
I weep with her?

Notes:

The legend of La Llorona, like all oral literature, varies, depending on the region and who is telling it.

1. "Oh, my children, my children..."
2. the river took them to straight to hell
3. the poor woman

The Comádres

O ne Mother's Day, my brother Eddie showed up at our kitchen door with a beautiful Pekingese pup. The little dog was tan, with little black smudges on his face, and looking like he had just smashed headlong into a wall, his two big, black eyes bugged out. Handing it to her, he said, "Happy Mother's Day, Mom." She looked tormented as she took the little bundle of fur into her arms.

"Ay, Eddie," she said in a pleading voice, *"Que voy hacer yo con este perro?"* It wasn't that Mom didn't like pets; on the contrary, what she didn't like is that they inevitably got sick and died. Few lived to die of old age. If it was not rabies, they got hit by a car, or disappeared and never came back. She was very sentimental about these things. Our yard was littered with gravesites for dogs and cats. But it didn't take long for Tiny, as she named him, to become my mom's pride and joy. Tiny was the only indoor dog we ever had.

Mom treated him like royalty. For many years he would be her loyal companion, so his death was especially hard on her. On payday she always bought him wieners and a box of Barnum's animal crackers, which he loved. She would send me to the store to buy beef bones so she could make him special *calditos*, or soups, unlike mutts before him that only got leftovers if they were lucky.

Each morning and evening she took Tiny for walks so he could do his *necesidades,* and she had a special cushion in the kitchen for him to sleep on. When the Fourth of July neared, she fretted because as soon as the fireworks began, Tiny would race under her bed and hide until they were over, after midnight. *"No seas verijón,"* she scolded him, *verijón* being an idiom for one with no balls.

Our yard was divided from our two neighbors' yards by open wire fences and side gates. One gate opened to my mother's *comadre* Doña Margarita's house, on the left, and the other to Doña Luisa's house, on the right. *"Ten, llevale esto a mi comadre Margarita,"* Mom would say, and I would dutifully take the plate or potful of beans or rice through the gate to deliver it. Usually, they would ask me to wait while they darted inside to return a clean plate from last time, or fill a new one with some treats to reciprocate with. *"Ten, dále esto a tu mamá."*

Many of the families in the barrio were *compadres,* godparents of one another's kids. For Mexicans, a *compadre* or a *comadre* was like family. It was a sacred bond. The fence to my Mom's comadre's yard was only about three feet high, making it easy for the two of them to *chismiar* or *comadriar.* The gossip usually centered on whose son was in jail, whose husband had beaten his wife, whose daughter had just gotten pregnant, and other pertinent barrio business. *"Como tal palo, tal astilla,"* they would both agree when a son or daughter turned out to be the unmistakable image of a no-good father or mother.

My mother's *comadre* was about four feet tall, a dark, stocky woman, whose face was pitted with dark brown scars from smallpox she had gotten as a child in Mexico, my mother explained. She was a generous lady who often joked with me. *"Como esta mi coloradito?"* she would say when she saw me in the yard. I hated the nickname, which meant something like "matchstick," referring to my red hair, which I also hated. She had a beautiful garden, but her specialty was the roses she grew in her front yard. She would prune them all the way back to the trunk, and I wondered how they would ever grow again, but in spring the bushes filled with huge, sweet-smelling roses.

But life between the two *comadres* was not always harmonious, and sometimes they had their spats; but after a few days they usually forgave one another with a peace offering, which I would carry through the gate. But something would come between them that might have divided them forever, but for the death of Tiny.

The day Tiny died, I buried him in a space between the almond and a quince, alongside the house. Mom wanted no part of it. She had lost a friend and took it hard. "Don't worry, Mom, I consoled. *Yo lo entierro,"* I said bravely. Though a teen myself, I was *the man of the house now*. My sisters and brothers had all left home, and Mom and I lived alone.

I wrapped the stiff, lifeless body in an old sheet and gently lowered Tiny into the hole. Now and then Mom watched from the living-room window. After burying him, I fashioned a head marker of old wood I found in the backyard, nailing a small cross at the top. I asked my mother for a photo of Tiny, cut it into an oval, set it under glass, glued it to the marker, and hand-lettered the name *Tiny* in an Old English style above it; finally, I placed a bouquet of flowers from our yard on the tomb.

When I was done, I called Mom, and she came out to see it. She stood there weeping openly and thanked me for the memorial. She was not an emotional person. It hurt me to see her cry. *"No llores, Mamá, Tiny ya está en el cielo."* Tiny was now in heaven, I assured her.

Ironically, at the time, my mother and her *comadre* were not on speaking terms. It had never been this bad. Weeks had passed, and neither had spoken a word. While I never knew what caused the row in the first place, it bothered me to see the rift between the two, especially now, when my mom could use compassion from her lifelong friend. Word had gotten out that Tiny had died, but I guess it was Doña Margarita's pride that kept her away. Worried, I told my mother one day, *"Tienes que perdonar a tu comadre, Mom."*

"Me, apologize to her? She's the one who needs to apologize to me!" Days passed, and the stalemate dragged on.

Meanwhile, the flowers I'd placed on Tiny's grave had wilted. Still the *comadres* did not speak. No matter how much I pleaded with my mom to make up with her *comadre,* she stoutly refused. She could be stubborn in the old Mexican way. But one day when she went out to tend Tiny's grave, she saw that a beautiful bouquet of roses had been placed there. I watched her through the living-room window. Though I could see only her back, I knew that she was crying.

Suddenly, she turned and walked briskly across her yard, through the side gate, and knocked on the backdoor of her *comadre's* house! I had never seen Mom walk with such determination. I stepped out to the kitchen porch, where I could watch. When her *comadre* opened the door, I heard voices, though I couldn't make out what they were saying, but I saw they were hugging one other. After a few minutes, my mother walked back through the gate, and I noticed a faint smile on her face, though she said nothing to me as she came inside the house. But one thing was clear: they would be *comadres* again. Tiny had reunited them from beyond the grave.

Un Nopál en la Frente

It became obvious to me early in life that the color of a person's skin would play a crucial role in succeeding in American culture. Ironically, in our family three of us—John, Shirley, and me—were born light-complected, with freckles and red hair. The other three—Mary, Eddie, and Jessie—were dark-skinned, with black hair. My mother would admonish me for playing in the sun. *"Métete a la sombra! Te vas a poner negro, como Indio!"* It was understood that to be a black or "dark Indian" was bad. The nice word for being dark-skinned was *moreno*.

Mexicans refer to light-skinned Mexicans as *güeros* or *güeritos*. I hated the word because it was often accompanied by a tone of ridicule. Where the red hair and freckles came from in our family, we never knew. Neither my mom nor dad had red hair, nor did their parents, as far as we knew, though my dad was light-skinned with freckles. I heard stories of Mexicans with blue eyes and fair skin in regions of Mexico, but I pretty much bought into the popular stereotype that all Mexicans were dark-skinned and had black hair, and that I was an anomaly.

When I became a dad years later, both of our boys were born dark-skinned, with jet black hair. When they asked, "Daddy, why do you have freckles?" I would say, joking, "One day my mother was painting the ceiling over my crib and I was spattered with drippings." They would crack up. "Tell it again, Dad, tell it again!

However, in school, being light-skinned gave me an advantage over my darker-skinned friends, who were quickly labeled slow learners and put in the back of the room. They were the ones prodded into fights by the White kids. As a result, they banned together, running in groups for self-protection. Ironically, most people never knew I was Mexican, and I could run comfortably in both circles, even with Whites from downtown. But this was risky business. None of us wanted to be called a *gringo lover.* "Check out this *vato.* He thinks he's better than us," they would say about any Mexican running with White guys.

But I have to admit something here. I had a *thing* for White girls, *gringitas,* as we called them in grammar school. I went head over heels for Greta Johnson and Louise Sailor, with the golden locks; but they never even knew I existed. My mother, sensing my dismay, would say in her sage wisdom, *"Acuerdate, amor de lejos, amor de pendejos,"* reminding me that love from a distance was a fool's love. *"Cuando te cáses, cásate con una Mexicana porque ellas saben como respetar a sus hombres."* It was only Mexican women who knew how to respect their men, so I needed to make sure to marry one, she warned. I would take her advice to heart years later and marry a girl from Mexico City.

It was the barrio culture for Mexicans to stick with Mexicans. Scandals would arise when someone married outside the group, a Mexican with a White, or the supreme disgrace, a Mexican with a Negro! These individuals were often ostracized in the barrio and treated with great suspicion. For a Mexican to pretend he was *better* than the rest was considered a supreme insult. *"Miralo, se cree muy Americano el pendejo, pero trae el nopál en la frente!"* The image of some idiot having a *nopál* (cactus) pasted on his forehead was hilarious. We all understood that the cactus was our firebrand, sealing our *Mexicanness,* something we could never disguise or change that we took to our grave. That no matter how *American* we thought ourselves to be, to *them* we would always be "just another Mexican" was an irony that too often proved to be true.

"You are not an American," one of my teachers once told me. "You're a Mexican."

"Mom, am I an American?"

"No, you are a *Mexican,*" she countered.

"But I was born here!" I protested. "And I speak English!"

"But in their eyes you will *always* be a Mexican." End of argument. The teachers also changed our names. Beautiful Spanish names were shortened, I suppose, for their convenience. Federico became *Fred,* Margarita became *Maggie*, Jose became Joe, and Richard became *Dick*. I hated *Dick*. We all knew what a *dick* was. Worse, were stories circulated in the barrio about Mexican families or individuals who had actually Anglicized their names, about the Campos who were now the Fields, and the Martinez who were now the Martins.

Our Spanish accent was a separate issue. No matter how hard they tried, many of my barrio buddies could never kick the Mexican accent, and it became a barrier to them. "Mai teechur, tol' me I gotta read dis' buk by tomurow." For me, shedding the accent was as easy as discarding an old coat. But there was a huge price tag for trading our mother tongue for another. We had to choose: Spanish or English; there would be no compromise. Being bilingual was not a thing touted in America in those days. "The sooner you get *rid* of Spanish and your accent, the better," was inherently understood by us Chicanos, pounded into our psyches to the point that some of us became *ashamed* to call ourselves Mexican. "No, I'm not Mexican, I'm *Spanish*!" we insisted. We understood clearly that *Spanish* had more *class* than the other word.

The advent of what would later be dubbed Pocho or Spanglish is even more of a mystery, but it neatly and easily embedded itself in the barrio, a tossed salad of English and Spanish. "Mi teacher me *dijo que tenia que* read *este* book y write *un* essay on it." There were no rules for grammar here. Nonetheless, most of us clearly understood it and we flowed between *las dos lenguas,* seamlessly.

And so we ate "Spanish food," not Mexican. My mom spoke Spanish only at home, though she understood and spoke some English. For her, to speak English was a cultural compromise . "Why should I?" she demanded. I was comfortable moving back and forth between the two languages and understood that one was to be used in barrio, and the other in public. I hated people scowling at us at a store or the bank when we spoke Spanish out loud, so I kept it to myself.

During the '40s it was not unheard of for families to forbid their children to speak Spanish in the home, believing that it would prevent them from getting ahead in American society. While this bothered me at the time, I understood why they were doing it; in our home it was not so. We all spoke flawless English, but we never forgot Spanish, though we spoke it brokenly. Many who lost the ability to speak Spanish would later grow to regret it, and I felt sorry for them.

For a Mexican born in the US, there was nothing more embarrassing or humiliating than to be spoken to in Spanish and not being able to answer! One of my mother's greatest dismays was that of the many grandchildren she had, not one of them spoke Spanish, with the exception of our son Michaelangelo, whom my wife and I ensured would grow up to speak Spanish, and she was proud of that.

Looking at myself in the mirror today, my red hair has grown white, and the freckles darkened, and my own *nopál en la frente* has almost vanished, though I still feel the prick of its spines on occasion. I had it removed surgically, so as to leave no scars. Now, I wear it proudly, by choice. After all, it cost me dearly.

Chicano Jaikus

Brown Dreamer #1
In a hot Desert borderland:
a rattler slithers over
bones of an illegal alien.

Brown Dreamer #2
Dried prunes on sand, a
Mexican family of five:
desert fodder now.

Brown Dreamer #3
To her plump belly,
Maria takes a sharp knife;
baby oozes out in land of plenty!

American Dream Recyled
Through the cylone fence
brown eyes gaze,
toward the Golden Arches.

La Llorona Revisited
In the cusp of night,
lament of a homeless mother:
"My babies, my babies, my babies."

Arabian Nights
A Mulsim mosque for
his headstone: Chicano falls
in far off Iraq.

Never Seem to Learn

Naive *gringo* there:
"Ah jus' *love* them hot peppers!"
Jalapeño strikes again!

Cultural Conflict

Pigskin:
We make footballs.
Mexicans make chicharrones!

Northern Delight

Hot from the stove:
a flour tortilla, butter
dripping from its ends.

Chicano Nightmare

Light-skinned Jose S
on the hot sandy beach, there—
squeezing Coppertone!

Hamburger Helper

Woolworth burger at
the counter; Jalapeño
from my mother's purse!

Supply and Demand

One bean burrito
for one baloney sandwich:
Even trade at lunch!

Language of the Barrio

I grew up believing that I spoke Spanish, since that was what we supposedly spoke at home. I say *supposedly* because the Spanish my mother taught us was the language of rural Mexico, which included many idioms. I would later come to learn that the Spanish spoken by middle- and upper-class Mexicans in Mexico is quite different, and that much of ours was either wrong, mispronounced, or didn't even exist in a Spanish dictionary.

My mother hated having to speak English, and I hated being her translator when we went to the bank or shopping. Everything took twice as long to do. The clerk would tell me something in English; I would translate it into Spanish for her, wait for her reply in Spanish, and then tell the man behind the counter what she had said! Translating was never easy because I often didn't know the Spanish or English word for something, and I would have to use hand signals while a line lengthened behind us and people began snickering.

Though I often found speaking Spanish a burden, I now cherish the ability to drift seamlessly between two languages. To certain people I could comfortably speak Spanish; to others, not. Sometimes, I spoke to them in English, and they would answer me in Spanish. Speaking sentences made up of part English and part Spanish was also normal to us. There were no rules for this. Often, an entire sentence was spoken in Spanish with only a verb or noun in English, and other sentences were mostly English with only a few Spanish words tossed in.

But most amusing was the language that developed by combining an odd mixture of English and Spanish. It was a language born out of necessity, the *hispanization* of English words, bastardized to fit a culture finding its way in a foreign world.

The way it worked was to make an English word *sound* Spanish either by its pronunciation, or by adding a Spanish-sounding prefix or a suffix to it. The trick was to make the word sound both like the English derivative and a Spanish word at the same time as in the phrase "to try", which became *el trai "tra-ee"!*

References to cars were among the best examples. A car became *el carro*. A truck became *la troka,* and a pickup, *el picóp.* Tires became *tallas "ta-yas",* rims became *los rines,* the clutch *el cloche,* and the brakes, *las brekas.*

Of course, the problem was that no real Mexican would have the slightest idea what we were talking about! *"A que la fregada, le tengo que componer las brecas a la troka, y pa' cabarla de chingar, se le ponchó una talla al carro."* To park became *parquiar,* and a parking lot, *el parquiadero.* A ride in a car was *un raite.*

References to money or currency abounded. A *quarter* became *una quada,* a dime, *un dáime,* and a nickel, *un nicle "neek-leh".* *"Oye, Compa, no traes cambio? Necesito unas quadas, daimes y nicles para parquiar."* It all made perfect sense to us in the barrio.

References to the home were affixed. A mop became *el mapa,* and to mop became *mapiar.* *"Ay muchacho, mira que cochinero me hiciste. Ahora voy a tener que mopiar todo el piso!"* To cook became *cuciar.* *"Ya me voy porque tengo que cuciar."* A cake was *un keki.*

The cannery became *la caneria,* the orchards or fields, *los files "fee-lehs",* and an irrigation ditch, *el dichi "dee-chee."*

References to undesirables were also used. A tramp was *un trampa,* and a drunkard, *un waino.* *"Cuando anden en el rio, tengan cuidado con los wainos y los trampas."* From *son-of-a-bitch* we wrought *sonovavichi.* Beer was sometimes called *birria,* which we later discovered is what Mexicans called goat meat!

We also adapted the names of department stores. *Montgomery Ward* became *La Mongomer,* and *Penny's, La Penny.* The movie house or *picture show* was *el cho.* *"Vamonos a La Penny, y a La Mongomer, y después al cho."*

A sweater was called *una sueda.* *"Necesito una sueda porque está haciendo mucho frio afuera."* A jacket was *la chaqueta."* Lipstick became *lipistiki,* and to apply it, *lipistiar*. To be very pretty was to be *muy pudi*. To be high-minded or high tone became *haitón* for men and *haitóna* for women. *"Mira nomas, se cree muy haitóna, la cabrona."*

Recently, after a long while of not seeing him, my wife said to our good friend Jose Montoya, a virtual repository of barrio slang, "There's something different about you, Jose. What is it?" Without the slightest pause, he replied, *"Oh, es que me eslimié,"* "es-sle-me-eh", a word he had clearly composed from the phrase *to slim down*. In jest, I still say to my wife, *"Vamonos a brekfestiar?"* as I ask her out to breakfast.

To this day, these words still creep into my vocabulary, though I have worked hard to learn the correct Spanish words for things. New words like those above have emerged and will probably keep emerging to accommodate an evolving language, especially in our world of computers and electronics. This was the language of the barrio, of a people cut off from their homeland and their mother tongue, adrift and searching for a port in a foreign land.

Yo Soy Latino

I am Latino; like a smooth glass of vino
I flow into your glass; I am Latino so
I gamble in Reno, maybe play
a little Keno, on the side, who knows.

Yo soy Latino, sharp, not like Jay Leno,
 pero como vino fino,[1] corked and aged,
sometimes caged, oft enraged,
a sage, page by page, the color beige.

I am a Latin lover from cover to cover,
better run for cover or I'll steal your lover,
a regular Valentino, Hollywood
lover boy; I kiss women half to death,
dissolve them with my stare, beware.

I am Latino, maybe even your *nino,*[2]
un *peregrino,*[3.] I soujourn through life
and all its strife; like a sharp knife I slice
real smooth and nice; I am the Latin dancer,
my hips naturally gyrate to the beat
of a cumbia, cha-cha-cha, or the rumba,
the mambo, the samba, the pasodoble,
with a Latin stroll; *una salsa movidita,*
suavecita, mi musica Latina, *muy fina,*
me mueve suave, como un ave.[4]

I am Latino, hot-blooded, hot tempered
hot like salsa, *pico pero bonito,*[5] spicy, *sabroso.*[6]
Steamy with emotions, the macho,
I must prove my manhood like the rooster,
the bull, *tanates*[7] swinging.
Los hombres no lloran,[8] men do not cry,
they just whimper; they simmer till they
explode like Mount Vesuvius, dubious.
I cry alone, in the dark.

Yo soy Latino, a state of mind
one of a kind, the world as seen
from behind, is square not round at all,
a suave Latino, *porque asi fue mi*
destino,[9] to be smooth, like aged *vino*
pull my cork, and I ooze blood,
deep crimson, *sangre Latina,*
que corre[10] deep, inside my veins.
It calls to me to me from afar:
Remember me? Remember me?

I am a relic *de tiempos pasados,*[11] refined by time,
like driftwood on a beach, within reach,
sanctificado;[12] a fossil from Europe,
Latin American, Latino Americano,
muy cercano,[13] donde *todos somos hermanos*[14]
brothers by speech, we reach
into the New World, a transplant from the old
oceans apart; like a work of art
I am painted on a canvas,
multicolored, multifaceted,
Latino, por el destino, como
un vaso de vino fino,[15] you
can drink me.

Notes:
1. but like fine wine
2. godfather
3. a sojourner, perigrine
4. dancing to Latin music, suave, smooth moving like a bird
5. I sting, but nicely
6. delicious
7. balls, testicles
8. Men don't cry
9. because that was my destiny
10. Latin blood that runs deep
11. from times past
12. sanctified
13. very close by, near
14. where we all are brothers
15. like a glass of fine wine

A True Rooster in Any Hen House Can Crow

My mother, despite having the equivalent of a fifth-grade education in Mexico, was a wit and a fountain of wisdom. While I sometimes scoffed at her country ways and ran aground of her Old World morals, one of the things I most recall about her was her mastery of Mexican *dichos,* old sayings, and she seemed to have one for each of life's encounters. Aside from the tried and true wisdom the *dichos* conveyed, their poignancy relied not only on their manner of delivery, but on their timeliness. To mean anything, each had to be delivered at a precise moment, just before or immediately after a life experience. Their humor, play of words, irony, and poetry brought me many a smile.

At the moment a young person learned a lesson the hard way after being told over and over by an adult, "Don't do it because you'll be sorry," she would say *"Ya vez, El Diablo no es diablo por Diablo, si no por viejo"* (The Devil is not crafty because he's the Devil, but because he's old!) When you spoke evil or gossiped about someone, she would quip, *"El que pa' arriba escupe en la cara le cai"* (Spit into the air, and it will fall back in your face). When you spoke foolishness, she warned, *"En boca cerrada, no entran moscas!"* (In a closed mouth, flies do not enter.)

When you fell in love with someone who never even bothered to look your way, she would shake her head and say, *"Amor de lejos, amor de pendejos"* (Love from a distance is a fool's love). One of her favorites was reserved for people who expected to be treated as special by others. *"De favor te abrázan, y ya quieres que te aprieten!"* (That person is doing you a favor by hugging you, yet you want them to squeeze!) Another variation she reserved for this condition was, *"Nada mas te dicen 'mi amor,' y ya quieres tu casa aparte!"* (No sooner does someone call you "my love," and already you want your own private living quarters!)

For the person who did favors for everybody else but neglected things in his own house, she scoffed, *"Candil de la calle, obscuridad de su casa!"* (A light in the streets, but in the home, darkness). When people began making excuses for failing to live up to things they bragged about doing, she mocked, *"El que es gallo, en cualquier gallinero canta!"* (A true rooster in any henhouse can crow!) For one who argued that while he may have been present at the scene of crime, he didn't actually *pull the trigger*, she would say, *"Tanto peca el que mata la vaca, como el que detiene la pata!"* (He who holds the cow by its leg, is as guilty as he who shoots it!) When you expected things would automatically get better by themselves, she said, *"Como se acuesta, asi se levanta."* (The person you are when you go to bed is the same person who rises the next day.)

These classic Mexican *dichos* were among her favorites. As a warning to be careful who your friends are: *"Dime con quien andas, y te dire quien eres"* (Tell me who you run with, and will tell you who you are). To admonish people who were wasteful, stingy, or hoarders, she said, *"Ni traga, ni deja tragar!"* (Look, he doesn't eat from his own plate, but refuses to let others eat from it too.) The word *tragar* here is another word for *comer* (to eat), but alludes to the kind of eating *dogs* or animals do, not humans. We had all seen a dog ignore his own bowl of food, but snarl at another dog that even gets close to it! When someone was heartless or cruel, she would say, *"Ojos que no ven, corazon que no siente"* (Eyes that cannot see, a heart that cannot feel).

For the person who lost out on something because others beat him/her to it, she said, *"El que tiene mas saliva, cóme mas pinóle!* (He who has the most saliva eats the most pinole!) Pinole is a crushed piñon powder that Mexicans are fond of, but a spoonful of it saps every bit of saliva from your mouth, causing you to sometimes choke! To fully appreciate the metaphor, you would have had to try the stuff yourself!

One *dicho* my mom seemed to use most was reserved for a person who had just failed at something he or she expected was simple or easy to do. She would mock, *"La vida no es enchilame otra!"* As with all languages, meanings and subtleties are lost in the translation, and this one meant something like, "Life is not as easy as ordering another taco with chile on it." That life is not a bowl of cherries has to be one of toughest lessons we must learn as humans.

My mom, you see, could crow in *any* hen house.

The Pálo

"He who loves his son will whip him often so that he may rejoice in the way he turns out."—Sirach, 30:1

The term *child abuse* was unheard of in the barrio. Justice to disobedient children was usually meted out by a father with a *nalgada,* a spanking with an open hand, or a *paliza* executed with a *palo* or tree branch, or worse, an ironing cord or a belt. *"Nomas esperate hasta que llegue to apa' del trabajo,"* mothers would warn. And we knew we were going to *get it* when our dads came home from work that night.

I'll never forget the "Whap! Whap! Whap!" of a belt or ironing cord coming down on the legs and butts of my friends, and their pitiful screams: *"No! No! No, Papá!"* And a father's obscenities as he vented his rage on a disobedient son: *"Muchacho cabrón! Ándale! Ándale! Ándale!"* It was a father's undisputed right to beat his own son without any interference from neighbors or the police. I respected my friends who took it *like men,* not even crying. The next day, they would brandish their welts and bruises like badges of valor. As for me, I was one big crybaby, with an abysmally low threshold for pain.

But all of my buddies then talked of getting *whuppin's* from their dads, so it wasn't just a *Mexican* thing. It was never questioned in those days; it was just the way things were done. But I had also seen it rage out of control by the brutal hand of a *macho* father who just seemed to get pleasure from beating his kids, or his wife, for that matter. Yet, even the beating of a wife was a man's private business, and few dared to interfere.

In the barrio, we never heard "time out" or "Go to your room," because most of us didn't even have a room of our own to go to! Our fear of the *paliza* kept us on the straight and narrow. When my mother left for work during the summers at Tillie Lewis cannery, she left me with a simple list of tasks: "Mow the lawn. Clean up your room. Feed the dog. Turn on the beans about two o'clock and put the burner on low and don't burn them!" She would get home about five thirty each day, sometimes on foot, or having caught a ride with someone else who lived in the barrio.

So because my father was absent in my life, it would be up to my mother to administer discipline. Though she was strict and ran a tight ship, she was fair, and I only "got it" when after several warnings I continued to disobey her simple rules.

Like a good son, I would put on the beans at two o'clock, just as she had instructed, calculating that I could sneak in a thirty-minute bike ride, or visit Robert or Charley to play a quick game of Monopoly, and still have plenty of time to rush back to add water to the beans. But just as Robert rolled a three that would put him on Park Place, where I had three hotels, I would leap up in terror. "What time is it!? Four o'clock? Oh shit, *the beans!*" And I would pump home as fast as I could to find smoke bellowing from the kitchen.

There are few smells worse than burnt beans, and there was no disguising it. The stench permeated the furniture, the curtains, and even the walls, lasting for hours, even if you opened all the doors and windows! "Damn! I forgot to mow the lawn, too!" She would usually let three or four of these transgressions pass with a simple warning: *"A la siguiente vas a ver!"* But after a few *next times* I would get it.

My mom had a wooden *palo* or stick she used for stirring the clothes inside the washing machine. It was about two inches wide, an inch thick, three feet long, and forked on one end. When the dreaded moment came, she would grab the *palo* and drag me into the kitchen. But before my *paliza* began, I would beg for mercy: "No! Mom, no! Mom, no! I'm sorry, I won't do it again!" But it was too late. I would even feign crying, but she just laughed. "I haven't even hit you yet!"

When the blows started, I assumed a defensive stance, like a boxer against the ropes, preparing for a barrage of body shots. "You really want something to cry about? I'll give you something to cry about!" She would scoff at my fake tears. "*Andale! Andale! Andale!*" and the thrashing began. In a feeble effort to protect my butt, I placed my open hands together behind my back, but the whacks stung my palms, which hurt just as badly. "*Para que aprendas a obedecérme!*" She was sullen afterward, and we didn't speak for a couple of days. I knew she had not enjoyed the episode, either.

Though I never thought about it consciously, when I had my two sons Miguel and Fernando later in life, I would instinctually defer to the *palo*. Early on, I made it clear to them that I descended from a *pálo* culture, and I would take no defiance or disrespect from them. A traditional Mexican woman, my wife expected *me* to discipline our boys and never interfered. But now that I was executioner, it never occurred to me that I would have to learn to control my anger or that I might seriously hurt them during the spanking; I could always stop myself, I believed. The guilt I felt afterward was debilitating. No one had ever even spoken about that.

Oddly, the old phrase, "Son, this is going to hurt me more, than it's going to hurt you," began to suddenly ring true, though I continued to scoff at all the silly talk about the *evils* of spanking, how it didn't work, about the psychological damage it caused, and how it would create another genera-tion of abusive children. For me, the *palo* was the only way I knew; it had worked for me, and it would work for my own sons.

However, it all ended one day after my youngest son Fernando, then about fourteen, had exhausted my patience. We were in the garage when I exploded at him. Looking around, I saw nothing I could use as a paddle, so I tore a thin wooden slat from the siding of a lightweight fruit box lying on the floor. I held him by the arm, and struck him over and over on his thighs. He started to wail in a way I had never heard before. "He's really putting on a good show, just like I used to," I concluded, and kept swinging. "Ow! Ow-ow! Dad, there's a nail in the board! A *nail*!"

In horror, I looked and saw two small nails protruding from the slat. My eyes welled with tears as I dropped it on the cement floor. My wife grabbed for him, holding him tight, and I reached out to hug him, too. "I'm sorry. I didn't know! I'm sorry," I repeated stupidly. Luckily, the nails were slightly bent and had penetrated his skin only superficially; but the reality that I could have seriously hurt him scared me.

This would be the last time I ever spanked either of my sons, though to this day, we all chuckle about it when I retell the story. Still, I can't help but wonder whether the spoiled kids of today wouldn't benefit from the resurgence of the old *palo*? I grew up just fine, and seem none the worse for it.

At Least You're Not in Jail

"At least you're not in jail," my mother would say when she had nothing really good to say about us. It was the absolute shame to a barrio family to have one of their kids wind up in jail. In those years, there was no gang stuff in Modesto, except for a few leftover *pachucos* or zoot-suiters who were older, tougher, *vatos, dudes* you didn't mess with. Sometimes they had a little blue cross tattooed on the flap of skin between the thumb and forefinger, with lines suggesting rays of light emanating from it. Some of the girls or *rucas*, as they were sometimes called, had the tiny cross tattooed on their foreheads. But we shared a kinship with them because we were *fellow Mexicans* in the same struggle, and we felt secure in having these warriors around for backup when things got rough. We called them *chingónes* (bad dudes).

We sometimes fought with *vatos* from other parts of town or with our rivals from "Tortilla Flat," as we jokingly called their barrio on the other side of Ninth Street. But the fights were usually one on one, bare-fisted, with no guns or knives. More commonly the physical rivalry took the form of a football or baseball game, and we *vatos* from "Juarez" always got our butts kicked by the Tortilla Flat *vatos*, since they were stronger and better athletes than we were, especially Frank Gonzalez. Frankie was a *Chicano Tarzan*, dark-skinned, handsome, muscular, with black shiny hair, and an amazing athlete. Then they had the Martinez brothers, Martin and Mike. Martin could throw a curveball that actually changed directions in midair! They also had the Hoyapotubi brothers, a Navajo family that had moved into their barrio. Nobody was as tough as they were. When one of the Hoyapotubis hit a ball, it disappeared into the horizon.

They liked hanging around with us, and I made sure I was their friend, especially Bobby who was my age. One night I took Bobby's older brother, Eric, with me to see my girlfriend, Ruby, who was babysitting at a home down the street from her place, and on the way back, her older brother who was lying in wait in the dimly lighted street, accosted us, thinking I was alone on the bike. When he realized that a Hoyapotubi was with me, and when Eric got off the bike and stood defiantly before him, his aggressiveness vanished! "Hey, how you guys doin? Where you headed?" Not a shot had been fired, as we headed back to the barrio.

Most of us never committed any crimes worthy of jail or prison time, and my worst offense was to steal gum or a candy from Long's Drugstore downtown. I never got caught, except for one time when a clerk stopped me from going out the door with a stupid corn-cob pipe I had pocketed. After a proper scolding by the manager, I was released with a warning: "I'm gonna have to call the cops next time." I felt ashamed for having done it.

One night, my friend Diego convinced me to help him steal a battery from a wrecking yard on Ninth Street near the river. Though I was scared, I went along to preserve my honor. I would be the getaway driver and lookout man. We pulled up behind the yard on a dirt service road, turned out the headlights, cut the engine, and slid to a stop. The plan was simple: "I'm gonna climb over the fence, get a battery, and toss it over the fence. We'll stash it in the trunk. You stay here and keep a lookout for the cops."

I was already shaking when Diego scaled the fence. Luckily, they had no guard dog. It was about ten o'clock, pitch dark and cold. Ten or fifteen minutes passed—nothing. Suddenly, in the rearview mirror, I saw the lights of a car pulling into the service road and coming toward us. "Oh shit, it's a patrol car!" I whispered out loud. The cop eased up alongside me, aiming a spotlight in my face. "Whadaya doing out here, son?" he asked, knowing I was up to no good. My mind raced to find a remotely logical answer and I blurted, "Uh … I'm waiting for my buddy who went to see his girlfriend at the trailer park." There was in fact, a trailer park nearby, alongside the river. I held my breath, hoping my lame answer would convince him. After a brief search of the car, the officer continued to eye me up and down, suspiciously.

I dreaded the thought that any minute now a battery would come flying over the top of the fence and land right at our feet! Had Diego even heard or seen the cop? We would surely go to prison for this! After a few tense moments, the cop warned, "Well, it's late, and you guys shouldn't be messing around out here."

"Yeah, uh … thanks, officer. I'll make sure we head directly home as soon as my buddy gets back."

"You do that." He got into his car and he drove off. "Oh shit, that was close," I mumbled to myself.

A few moments later, Diego crawled back over the fence, without a battery. "Damn, that was close," he said. We both slinked back into the car and back to the barrio in utter failure. "What a dumbass idea," I told my friend, who sat in silence. As I lay in bed, Mom's words *at least you're not in jail* haunted my dreams that night.

But a more serious scrape with the law actually got me locked up in Juvenile Hall for a weekend. "Curley", one of my high school buddies, was an unsightly Oakie, about six feet two inches tall, who wore coke-bottom glasses and had a face pockmarked by pimples and blackheads. He had slick, straight hair, which is why I sarcastically dubbed him "Curly." He drove a slick, "raked" (lowered in the front), metallic blue '49 Merc, with a white Naugahyde interior he had gotten done in Tijuana. The "pap-pap-pa-pa-pap-pap" of dual glasspack mufflers turned everyone's heads when he revved up the engine or downshifted from third gear to second at every stoplight, cruising Tenth Street on Friday and Saturday nights, especially after the football games. The girls went ape over his car, and his pipes too.

One day, Curly announced that he wanted a set of moon hubcaps for his car. We scouted a place in north Modesto, where he had earlier spotted a set. The car was parked in a driveway, and it appeared dark inside the house. It was about ten at night, and, deeming that no one was home or the occupants asleep, we eased up behind the car and left the engine idling while Curly went around the driver's side and I kneeled at the passenger side and we each began prying off the caps with screwdrivers. However, the caps screeched loudly with each pry and were much harder to remove than we had anticipated. "Hurry up, hurry up!" He moaned in frustration.

Suddenly the porch light came on, and a man scrambled out of the house. "Hey! What the hell are you guys doing?!" In a heat of panic, Curly dashed to his car, jumped in, and sped off without me! His tires squealed as he peeled out, and I could smell the burned rubber. I started running, not sure where to go. I could not believe Curly had abandoned me. Then an awful chorus of barking dogs began. I had never heard so many dogs! I ran wildly into the night. Seeing a dark house with no gates, I slipped into a backyard and cringed behind a large rose bush and waited, completely out of breath.

Within moments a couple of patrol cars arrived! I could hear the squawk of police radios and see their spotlights darting back and forth at the houses along the street. About fifteen minutes passed, and I was beginning to think maybe I had escaped, but how was I going to reconnect with Curly? How would he find me? It was a long walk back to my house in the barrio across town. Just then I heard footsteps and was blinded by a flashlight beam as an officer spotted me.

The jig was up. I was going to prison for sure. "Alright, young man, come on out of there!" he commanded. I came out with my hands up, just like in the movies. He cuffed me and placed me into the backseat of his patrol car. I don't even remember the long ride to the juvenile detention center or being booked, for that matter. All I could think of was, "Mom is going to kill me!"

As I sat in my cell that night, I felt both relieved and outraged—outraged that Curly had gotten away, leaving me to take the rap! I was relieved the ordeal was over. The next day my brother Jesse came to see me. He had the manner of a seasoned veteran, and when he spoke, he always made a brutal kind of sense to me, cutting to the chase. "Mom is really hurt," he began, nodding his head in disbelief. "Damn, brother, if you're going to steal, why don't you steal something worthwhile? *Hubcaps?* Shit!" To this day, I have never forgotten his words.

I was released on a Sunday, after a brisk scolding by the judge, who told me that this would not go on my record, since it was my first offense. "Better watch who you're running around with." Funny, that's exactly what my high school counselor had said to me when I had gotten into trouble for ditching school some time earlier. I never spoke to Curley again, and, barring the exception of parking tickets, this would be my last brush with the law.

On the way home, I couldn't help but snicker to myself about why the cops had made such a big fuss about stealing hubcaps, when I had heard of kids actually stealing the whole damned car, only to get a free ride home in a patrol car and a warning to their parents for what was then called joyriding!

When Jesse and I got home, my mother was sullen. There were no accusations, no scolding; no *paliza*, yet I knew by her demeanor that I had disappointed her terribly. I had shamed her among the other mothers in the barrio. She would no longer be able say of her son, "At least he's not in jail."

The Term Paper

I t was 1956 when my high school junior composition teacher assigned my first term paper, on a subject of our own choosing. I scrambled in terror to read the guidelines for the assignment: library research, citations, footnotes, and a bibliography! It seemed overwhelming. I was doomed, an F or D paper, for sure. Though I was familiar with libraries and an avid reader, I had never written a research paper.

As the due date loomed, I forced myself to choose a topic. Since I was of Mexican descent, maybe I would choose something about Mexico. I loved art, so maybe I could also choose something to do with that. It made sense. After finding listings for art books in the old card catalogue, I came to one dog-eared card listing a book, titled *Los Tres Grandes* (The Three Great Ones), about three of Mexico's greatest muralists. I had never even known Mexico *had* great artists!

When I began to browse the vivid color plates of their murals, I was amazed. I had never seen art like this. At this point in my life, I was under the impression that a painting was supposed to depict something "pretty": an ocean beach, a tree, a stream, mountains, an old barn, an old boat— something that would match your carpet and hang over a couch.

This art, however, conveyed the immense suffering of Mexico's poor, the plight of its working class, and the abuse of Indians at the hand of oppressors, conquistadores, politicians, and "fat politicos." No one, not even priests, was spared by these muralists' brushes and paint. It was damning. It was not a personal art but a public one, displayed on giant walls and ceilings for everyone to see!

I was even more amazed when I began to read the text telling of the incredible lives and sacrifices of these artists, humiliated and disgraced in their own time because they negated European and salon art in an effort to create a *Mexican* art. My world was shaken. How was the mind of this freckled little barrio boy to take all this in?

Worse, was this even an acceptable topic to write about? "My teacher will probably hate it," I convinced myself. But time was the enemy. Already a couple of weeks had passed, and I had to choose something now, or I would never get my essay done!

So on my little three-by-five cards I dutifully copied significant quotes from the text, their page numbers, the author's name, the book's title, publishing company, and date of publication, and, following the teacher's strict guidelines, I set out to compose my first term paper, titled, "Mexico's Three Great Ones."

It was not as hard as I had thought. I had plenty to write about as I took each artist—Diego Rivera, David Alfaro Siqueiros, and Jose Clemente Orozco—and wrote about each one. On the day the paper was due, I sheepishly handed it in, as did the rest of my classmates. I purposely slid it to the bottom of the pile. It would be a disaster; I knew it. But I would be happy if I got at least a C- on it, like most of my peers.

On the day the papers were to be returned the students nervously fidgeted. I braced for my F. "Class," the teacher announced, "as you all know, I have your essays graded, but before I hand them back, there is one paper that I want to read to you." We hushed. "The paper is titled 'Mexico's Three Great Ones.' I sank in my seat! My ears flushed. "God, please don't let her reveal my name," I prayed.

She proceeded to read *my essay*! When she finished, my ears were still ringing. "Now this, class, is an example of what a term paper should be." She handed the essay to me, and, looking my way, my classmates began to clap. I turned beet red.

Though I had been at the top of my class in other subjects, writing had not been one of them. I had no idea I could write, but I had secretly enjoyed it. At that moment, no one, including myself, could have possibly guessed I would master the art of writing research papers in college and, in a twisted quirk of fate, go on to become an English teacher myself. I would later quip to my own students "things have gotten so bad in America that now they have *Mexicans* teaching you how to speak and write English correctly!"

Even more importantly, I had discovered something vital about myself. I too was *Mexican,* and in some way, these artists and the people they painted were *my people, my roots*, and this was certainly nothing to be ashamed about. In the years that followed, I made several pilgrimages to Mexico, and I would see the murals of Siqueiros, Orozco, and Rivera for myself, and be dazzled all the more by their incredible works.

That term-paper assignment would be the first in a series of important changes in my life, which would result in my becoming a Chicano/Mexican studies professor at a community college in 1972.

Para los Tres Grandes (For the Three Great Ones)

Gracias, Diego,[1]
for your brush that showed his dignity
to the bigoted masses for whom an *Indio*
was subhuman—*"un Indio pata rajada"*[2]—
and the grandeur of *Tenochtitlan,*[3]
with its magnificent marketplaces, canals, and palaces,
the Constantinople of the Americas, Cortez said.

You painted him small in stature, dark,
almost hideous, standing alongside the pale,
white Europeans who towered over him—
who called him an *Indian, "gente sin razon."*[4]
In hues of brown, rust, umber (burnt and raw),
yellow ochre, a terra cotta red man
with a hooked nose—yet a nobility
emanates from his burnt sienna frame.

We can feel the rage of your brush, in your
condemnation of the envy, greed, and avarice
of the priests, entrepreneurs, and conquistadores;
vultures in wolve's clothing, birds of prey,
carrion creatures and bloodsuckers, readying
to extract the very life from creatures
they said God created to be dominated.

You painted him hanging from the trees,
whipped and beaten into submission, driven

like oxen to cultivate the very land stolen from him;
and you endured the ire and insults of the *rubios:*[5]
upper classes who detested this shameful exposition
on public walls of this genocide of brown men, this holocaust
of the Americas—this contemptuous stain on Mexico.

Gracias tambien,[6] David Alfaro Siqueiros,[7]
for your portrayal of the atrocities commited
against this redman of the Americas, acts done
in the name of decency, in the name of progress;
in the name of God.

Who cannot feel
the agony of Cuahtemoc,[8] tied to a slab of stone,
and his fear of the vicious dogs baring their fangs,
as conquistadóres in steel torch his feet
to force him to confess where the gold was hidden.
His eyes reek with torment: "Do you think I am on a bed of roses?"
he tells a countryman
who cries out in pain alongside him.

Your figures leap out from the walls, plunging
at us, defying gravity, defying perspective;
you weren't satisfied with flat figures of two
dimensions only; yours were to be looked up at,
or down on, and your brushstrokes were those
of a calculated madman, deftly pushing paint
to its limits, heaping it in gobs, not cleanly, like Diego.

But it's in the eyes, David, that you captured
the pain; they are deep, black, glossy eyes, victims
of the fat politicos, the politcal *coyotes*, who stole
what was not theirs, the eyes of those who bravely
fought oppression with sticks, rocks, and machetes:
the Pancho Villas,[9] Benito Juarezes,[10] Miguel Hidalgos,[11]

the Moreloses,[12] and Emiliano Zapatas[13] laying down
their lives for generations yet to be born.

You too, made public what should have been
kept in darkness, in the shadows, and you created
an art that was purely Mexican, like beans,
like tequila, like the maguey, like the tortilla,
not salon art—pretty, calculated, orderly,
with vases of pretty flowers, apples on a plate—
but an art of war, of revolution, and of justice.

Gracias tambien, Jose Clemente Orozco,[14]
for the fire in your work, for the thrusting
bayonets, the legions of marching soldiers
winding their way through battlefields
of chemical gas: modern genocide,
while men in tails and tophats drink toasts to the stockmarket;
surrounded by grinning,
toothless prostitutes wearing gold rings.
Campesinos[15] struggle mercilessly against
an angry sky, a barren landscape of magueys
stabs the sky; men of all stations contorted,
distorted, misshapen; a Franciscan priest
leans in to kiss a leper. You were angry,
you were offended, you were tormented,
and you forced us to see death in all its shapes
and sizes: in science and technology designed for killing.
In Goyaesque[16] fashion, you showed us Disasters
of War,[17] the agony of broken, pierced bodies,
the rape of Latin America, a torment of
the masses, in blacks, and reds, crimson
and black, trampling of the natives under-
foot, your brush a weapon, a knife, slashing
at the swine-faced politicos counting their
blood money, squeezed from veins of the poor.

"A work of art is never negative. Being a
work of art makes it constructive," you said.
Yes, *ustedes tres grandes*, redefined art,
turning it into a weapon against
complacency, ignorance, myths, and lies.
Gracias, compadres, though your work shames
and humbles us, we sing to you: *"Estas son
las mananitas, que cantaba el Rey David...."*[18]

Notes:

1. Diego Rivera, great Mexican Muralist (1886-1957)
2. "indio pata rajada," disparaging term for the Indians of Mexico: "one with cracked feet"
3. what Mexico City was called before the Spanish Conquest of Mexico in 1519
4. a people without reason, or logic
5. blonde, light-skinned
6. "thank you, too"
7. David Alfaro Siquieros, Mexican Muralist (1898–1960)
8. last King of The Aztecs; he surrendered to Cortez in 1521
9. famous general who led troops in northern Mexico against the government in the Mexican Revolution (1910–20)
10. first Indian President of Mexico, who wrote Mexico's constitution
11. priest who led the War of Independence in 1810
12. a priest who led forces in southern Mexico in the War of Independence
13. famous leader from southern Mexico in Mexican Revolution
14. Mexican muralist (1883–1949)
15. farmworkers
16. Francisco Goya, Spanish artist (1746–1828)
17. series of etchings on the Spanish Civil War done by Goya
18. lyrics to Mexican birthday song

Never Forget You Are Mexican

I don't know how I got the crazy notion as a kid that I wanted to be an artist when I grew up. "Whatcha doin', Richard?" Robert would call.

"Nuthin', you?"

"Nuthin'."

"Wanna draw?"

"OK." And we would sit for hours on our kitchen table or his and draw characters from old comic books: Superman, Spider-Man, Mickey Mouse, Donald Duck, and Dick Tracy. When I told my mom that I wanted to be an artist, she just laughed. "Why? Be something worthwhile like a doctor or a lawyer. Artists don't become famous till after they're dead." How this simple, uneducated mother knew this, I'll never know.

I liked school, though my mother never pushed me. I was always at the top of my class, and all my teachers liked me. As soon as they discovered I was good at art, I would be given special tasks like making posters and decorations for the bulletin boards. This would continue until junior high school, when I started to rebel and act up. My behavior worsened when I got into high school and started running with the wrong crowd, ditching school, and shoplifting in downtown Modesto.

Early on, I became an avid reader of novels such as *Treasure Island*, *The Adventures of Robin Hood*, *Black Beauty*, *Chief Black Hawk*, *Last of the Mohicans*, *Call of the Wild*, and *The Black Stallion*. The school library and McHenry Library in downtown Modesto became my second homes. I loved even the smell of books. We had no books at home, with the exception of some my brother John found in a cardboard box at the city dump. Mom kept it under her bed. I loved to slide it out and graze through the hodge-podge of books inside, but my favorites were Webster's Dictionary and a couple of encyclopedias, one that contained beautiful colored plates of animals, plants, and birds in it. I spent hours drawing from it.

In high school I began to win prizes in art contests and competitions, taking numerous first, second, and honorable mention awards. But when I excitedly showed Mom the ribbons, medals, and certificates, she would mumble sarcastically, "*Y para que sirven estas garras? Porque no te dan dinero?*"It angered me that she saw no value in medals or ribbons, which she referred to as "*garras*", or "rags." Instead, she demanded to know why I was never awarded money!

It's almost funny, now that I think of it, that nowhere along the way did any teacher or counselor ever speak to me about the possibility of going to college. No one I knew ever went to college, especially the Mexican kids from the barrio. Most dropped out, got a job, got married, and started having kids. That was it. Little did I know then, but my artistic talents would be the key to a college education. In high school, most Mexican kids were sent straight to the school's auto body shop, and the girls to home economics classes.

But I signed up for every art class the school offered! Mrs. Barnett and Mr. Thorsted, my high school art teachers, began to lavish me with praise. At Mr. Thorsted's insistence, I entered the annual AAA Safety Poster contest in 1956, as part of a class project. But when I was told I had taken first place, and that my poster would be printed and distributed nationwide, that became the turning point for me. The adulation and respect I got from my peers was daunting. I was a celebrity! Everyone congratulated me in the hallways, even students who had never spoken to me before! One day soon after this, Mr. Thorsted asked me to stay after class. "Richard, I want you to think about going to college," he said with great conviction. I was shaken. Me? College? The idea had never even entered my mind! When I told Mom that my teacher wanted me to go to college, she hardly reacted as I had expected. "*Estas loco?* Where did you get such a crazy idea?" she asked with dismay. "College costs money. We are poor. Besides, Mexicans in this country are always on the *bottom;* ask me, I know."

"But my art teacher said I should go."

With disgust, she retorted, "He is just lying to you."

Regardless, Mrs. Barnett and Mr. Thorsted worked hard to make connections with the dean of California College of Arts and Crafts, in Oakland, even taking me to the campus on their own time, with their own money, to meet with Carol Purdy, design teacher and dean, a lovely old woman who looked me straight in the eye, squeezed my hand hard, and said, "Don't worry, my dear. You will do well here."

The final year in high school was spent preparing a portfolio representative of my work, drawings, designs, and paintings to be submitted for a scholarship competition for incoming students. I was elated when I found out I had been given a full scholarship for the first year. With the help of my art teachers, I began applying for other local scholarships, and was awarded several, including one from Bank of America for $500 dollars! That would almost pay for a semester's tuition, which at the time was $600, extravagant, especially for a kid from a barrio.

Meanwhile, my mom resigned herself to my decision. I was the last of her brood. The rest had all married, moved away, had kids, and were busy living their lives. "I don't understand why you can't be like your brothers and sisters, get a job, get married, and settle down," she muttered. But marriage was the last thing on my mind. I began to think this was the real reason she didn't want me to go; she would be alone now. But I wanted so badly to prove her wrong: *Mexicans* could make it. I would.

One day, when our neighbor's sister and her daughter were visiting from Oakland, it occurred to my mother to ask if they might have an extra room they could rent to me. It turned out they did, a small attic loft, which they graciously offered to me free of cost! Things were falling into place.

I had just purchased my first car about that time, a 1947 Plymouth, from a mechanic who had just put a rebuilt engine in it. This would serve as transportation in my new world.

It was the late summer of 1957, and the date for my departure neared. As I packed my bags, my mother watched solemnly, often voicing the same concerns she had when I first told her I wanted to go to college. *"No tienes dinero. Como vas a pagar la renta? Quien te va cocinar? Quien te va a lavar tus calsones?"* She simply could not understand how I would pay the rent; who would cook for me, and who would wash my underwear?

My mom and I had never been touchy-touchy kind of people. I had never kissed her, and she had never kissed me. I had never told her I loved her, nor had she to me. In fact, we had never even held hands, or hugged one another. That was the old *Mexican* way. These things were unnecessary. Nonetheless, the moment of my departure was supremely awkward.

It was early August, when the two of us stood there, on that rickety old porch, staring down at the floor, not knowing what to do or say. I had expected some words of encouragement, well wishes, or for sure a blessing, but what she said took me completely by surprise.

We managed an awkward embrace. I got in the car, fighting back tears, and as I started the engine, she leaned into the window. *"Never forget you are a Mexican,"* she commanded solemnly.

"I won't, Mom," I promised, and, with the resolve of a heady eighteen-year-old and thirty dollars in my pocket, I slowly backed out of our dirt driveway and drove off. In the rearview mirror, I could see Mom standing there, so small and alone, watching her last son leave home.

I would go to college and prove to her wrong about Mexicans. This one would be on top, not at the bottom like she said; I just *knew* it. . Each year I continued to apply for scholarships, and that way was able to pay for my entire college education. In 1962, I was elected student body president and chosen to be valedictorian at my graduation. Mom was in the audience as I received my bachelor's degree in art—my mother, who had never once come to one of my previous graduations or open houses, sitting there, proudly. How could this simple, emigrant mother even dare dream that one of her children would one day graduate from college? We hugged openly that day.

I would go on to receive a master's degree a year and a half later. But in the process, I had forgotten the promise I had made to her when I left for college that day: I had forgotten I was *Mexican*! It was not until the early 1970s and the advent of the Chicano Movement that I would *rediscover* my heritage, and the full meaning of her words *Never forget you are Mexican* would dawn on me. I could proudly say to her now, "Don't worry, Mom, I won't ever forget I am Mexican."

Two Distinct Visions

I. The First View

Dawn from the back of a truck.
I'm standing atop a twelve-foot ladder;
I'm sixteen and it's a hundred degrees at noon.
Peach fuzz, pasted on my neck, burns.
Twenty-five cents a bucket, five bucks for a hard day's work;
Contratista[1] throws out half the damned box:
too small, too green, too ripe.
Wetbacks beat me to a better set;
I'm stuck with four lousy trees.
Straps cut into my shoulder;
the ladder slips and I fall with a full bucket!
A hornet's nest and a black widow spider
hide in the branches. Deathlike sleep
at night heralds my future.

II. The Second View

I stand at the apex of the Pyramid of the Sun
in Teotihuacán, Mexico, in the rain-soaked
Valley of Anáhuac, or the steps to the temple
of Tula[2], or peering down from Monte Alban,[3]
running my hands along the exquisite stonework
at the temples of Mitla;[4] or peering down
from the pyramids of Uxmal[5] and Chichen-Itza[6]
into the verdant jungles of the hot, humid Yucatán.
I'm on the pyramid at Tulúm[7] transfixed by the

115

turquoise waters of the Caribbean, or hypnotized
by emerald depths of a Centóte,[8] keeper of the bones,
pointing me clearly to where it is I've come from .

Notes
1. a farm labor contractor
2. pre-Columbian Toltec ruins in central Mexico
3. pre-Columbian Zapotec ruins in Oaxaca, Mexico
4. pre-Columbian Mixtec ruins in Oaxaca, Mexico
5. pre-Columbian Mayan pyramid in Merida, Mexico
6. pre-Columbian Maya center in southern Yucatan
7. pre-Columbian Mayan ruins in Qunitana Roo, Mexico
8. underground wells found throughout the Yucatan peninsula where
   the Maya once conducted religious sacrifices

The Coffee Can

I've had a few beers today to celebrate my discharge from three long years in the army. My mom was happy to see me when I came home the other day, after two and half years in Germany. I called her from San Francisco International:"Mom, put on the beans and warm up some tortillas. I'll be there in a couple of hours!" She prayed to the Virgin for my safe return. It is 1965. Already the barrio is changed. Some houses have been leveled and converted to parking lots for semi-trucks. A new freeway, Highway 5, has been built, skirting downtown, cutting Modesto in half! I look for my pals Charlie and Raul, but they've married and moved across town. I stop by Robert's house but he's married and moved away. What else is new? I have no idea. I should get a job, but not just yet. I think I'll go back to Oakland. There's nothing left for me in Modesto, and the barrio seems dead. I grab another beer from the refrig. "I'll be right back Mom, I'm going downtown."

"No te tardes."

"No, I won't be late."

I have only memory of my dad at home. What little else I know about him was told to me by my mother: how he loved to drink and party, how he had a beautiful voice and everyone wanted him to sing, how he was popular with the ladies, and how he abused her when he came home drunk in the early hours of the morning, dragging her out of bed so she could cook for him and his drinking buddies. One day, when she could take no more, *"Lo heché a la calle con todi' sus garras"*, she would boast, describing how threw him, along with his "rags," out into the street, sometime about 1942, when I was about three. She was a tough woman. She would need to be, to raise her six kids by herself. My brother Jesse quips to this day, "If mom was a boxer in Joe Lewis's time, Lewis would not have been champ!"

I find myself at St. Stanislaus Cemetery out on Scenic Drive in Modesto. I care-fully weave my way between the plots. I hate the idea of stepping on a dead people. I head in the general direction I believe it to be. It's been years since I've been here; in fact, since his funeral in 1953. I was never sure what he died of, but I knew it had something to do with his drinking. "It's close to a faucet," I remind myself, as I stag-ger from headstone to headstone. I find the faucet, but the plot is nowhere in sight. "Shit, I know it's here someplace." I search for the name. It has a photo of him on it, I suddenly recall. Making it even harder is the fact I am a little drunk. In fact, I am carrying a half-full can of Schlitz.

In that one memory, he and I were eating beans in our rickety kitchen on Flores Avenue. I was sitting on his lap, and he was showing me how to tear a tortilla into small triangles and use them to scoop up the beans, Mexican style. I don't recall using silverware to eat with until I started school or when we ate in restaurants downtown.

I go back to the faucet as a reference point and start again. Jacinto, oh Jacinto, where the hell are you? I take a slug of beer and plod on. I am determined to find him.

Jacinto Rios was born in Panuco, Zacatecas. How he wound up in Torreon where he met my mom is lost to history. Mom always talked of her impoverished childhood. *"Eramos pobres,"* she would repeat. She married Jacinto at age fifteen, and a year later gave birth to my brother Juan. She often spoke of the misery of life in Mexico after the Mexican Revolution of 1910–1920. She wanted more. She wanted a better life. So about 1923, at the insistence of my mother, the two emigrated to the US, and Jacinto got a job working in coal mine in New Mexico, where my sister Shirley was born. He despised it, and they returned to Mexico.

But life in Mexico did not improve for them, and Mom continued to insist they return to the US. Meanwhile Mom had given birth to my sec-ond sister, Mary. But one day, as my mother slept with her new baby, she woke to find a scorpion next to her cheek! In an act of motherly protec-tion, she squashed it. That did it. She went up to my father and announced, "I'm returning to the United States. If you want to come with us, fine. If not, we're going without you!" Her mother and two sisters were already living in Modesto. Moreover, my dad's sister, Juana, lived in the barrio there, too. Jacinto relented; he had little choice.

"Damn, here it is!" I finally find it, nowhere near where I remember it to be. For courage, I take another swig of beer. It's September and hot. For a couple of minutes, I stand there, staring at the headstone, then sit on the unkempt lawn facing it. I look around to see if anyone is looking. Nobody. A crow cackles from a nearby pine tree. Across the street, I see the Stanislaus County Hospital where, as my mother liked to put it, "dejaste tu ombligo" (you left your umbilical cord), I was born. The name on the stone reads "Jacinto Rios, 1899–1953."

"Necesitas zapatos. Ve con tu Papá y dile que te de dinero pa' que te compres unos nuevos," I would hear Mom telling me to find my father and ask him for money to buy a new pair of shoes. He lived in a small railroad section house on Seventh Street. Across the street was Fajardo's bar, an old dive where he often hung out. I hated that part. I was about twelve years old. Standing at the door of the *cantina*, I waited for a surge of courage, and then bolted inside. Wading through the stench of beer and cigarettes, I would find him perched on a stool, drinking beer with his cronies. *"Que quieres?"* he would brusquely ask me as I looked up at him. He already knew why I had come.

I keep staring at the headstone. I remember I never cried at his funeral and how guilty I felt about it. My mood changes. I wish I had known him. I never had a dad. I begin to think of how lucky my friends Robert, Charlie, and Raul are. They have real fathers. I am overtaken by a surge of anger. I am mad at him for abandoning us. I light a Pall Mall and take a drag, and another sip of beer. I begin to feel good. I have a buzz.

"Que quieres? Zapatos? No tengo dinero! Andale y dile a tu mamá que no tengo dinero y que te los compre ella!" he would say in a mock angry tone, turning to his pals for approval. I was not about to walk all the way home to tell my mother he said he had no money and for her to buy the shoes for me; plus I *knew* he was just playing with me. With a dumb grin, he would shove his hands into his pocket and pull out a five. *"Es mi hijo,"* he would boast to his *borracho* friends. "Gracias, Papa," I would mutter and head downtown to Thom McAnn's Shoes to buy myself a new pair of shoes.

As I sit here in silence, the anger I feel begins to dissipate; it's replaced with something like sympathy, like compassion. I want to speak out loud, but what if someone hears me? Is it normal to talk to the dead? Tender thoughts invade me. "Maybe you weren't such I bad man, Papá. You were just a product of your times, like all Mexican men: mean, tough, a macho." I "field strip" the Pall Mall and take another swig of Schlitz. It's almost empty now.

I don't remember whether he called or wrote to let me know it was time to go for the coffee can. I walked up Hosmer Street, across the Southern Pacific tracks, and down the other side to Seventh Street. About half a mile up was the old Seventh Street Bridge that crossed over the Tuolumne River, toward downtown Modesto. Two large cement lions guarded both entrances to the bridge. I always paused midway for a few minutes to contemplate the river below. About another half mile on the right was the section house where my dad lived, which provided housing for the railroad workers. It was a cramped, one-bedroom apartment. My father invited me in, and we would talk for a few minutes. *"Coma esta tu mamá? Tus hermanos? Hermanas?"* he would ask, as if he genuinely cared about us. "Fine, fine, we're all fine." Then, he would open his closet and pull out a coffee can full of pennies, handing it to me.

I suddenly begin to talk out loud to him. "Papá, I wish I had known you. I'm sorry I didn't cry at your funeral. I've just been discharged from the army a few weeks ago. I went to Europe. I went to college. I know you treated Mom badly, and I've hated you all these years for it."

You can't possibly imagine how heavy a one-pound can of pennies is! I would tuck it snugly under my right arm first, since it was the strongest. *"Gracias, Papa,"* I would say as I headed down Seventh Street, back to the barrio. About every block, I would stop to change arms. By the time I reached bridge, I was famished. At each entrance of the bridge, underneath the lions, were cement benches, where I rested for about twenty minutes, gathering strength for the second half of the trip back home.

I babble on about this and that. I am comfortable talking now. The buzz from the beer makes me even more nostalgic, almost giddy. I don't care if anyone sees me now. After all, I am a young man visiting his dad's grave. Regardless of my hatred for this man, I know he is my father. The man who was partly responsible for my being here on earth, right? And I've turned out alright, even without a dad. I smile at the easy flow of my thoughts. The sun is beginning to set. I've been here how long? An hour?

My mom would put the coffee can full of pennies inside cupboard in our kitchen, right next to the cod liver oil she forced me to drink every day. "Quick, bite down on the slice of orange!" She commanded as I downed the atrocious liquid, in my heart believing that Mom knew best. "It's good for you," she said, chuckling. The opening of the cupboard was covered by a curtain my mom had made from an old flour sack. Each day in grammar school, she would count out seven pennies from the coffee can, tie them into a small knot on corner of a handkerchief, and repeat, "Now, don't lose this. It's for your milk." That's exactly what the little milk carton cost at the school's cafeteria.

Sometimes, I would sneak a handful of pennies to buy a Pepsi or some sunflower seeds at Lupe and Abe's store on Ninth Street. Other times, I lugged out the can and placed it on the kitchen table. Grabbing fistfuls of pennies, I let them sift through my fingers back into the can. I loved the metallic "tinkle" they made in those days, not the dead, leaden thud they now make. "I'm rich! Rich!" I would think to myself.

It's beginning to get dark. I finish off the beer. I've sobered up a little, and the buzz has worn off. I stand up and pause to look one last time at the faded picture of Jacinto Rios. He's wearing a hat. There's no smile on his face. "You know, Dad," I say out of nowhere, "despite the terrible things you did to Mom and to us, I want you know I forgive you for it. Thank you for giving me the gift of life." I turn, crumple the empty beer can in my hand, and toss it into a trash can nearby. I walk away and don't look back.

The Mánda

In the weeks that followed, I wandered around Modesto aimlessly. I looked up a couple of old high school buddies, an old flame or two, but they had all moved on. Here I was, twenty-six, single, holding a master's degree in art, and honorably discharged from military duty, with a good-sized wad of mustering-out pay and money I had invested in savings bonds for three years. But I had no real plans for my future. With no real possibility of surviving on my art, maybe I could try a little teaching? I always had a job as a florist no matter where I went, since this is the way I had supported myself through college. Meanwhile, I'd visit with my mom and hang around the barrio for a while. But my heart was in the Bay Area: Oakland, Berkeley, and San Francisco. Nothing compared to that. "I'll hang around here for a couple of weeks, and then head back to Oakland," I convinced myself.

Sensing this, "*Sientate*," my mother said to me one day. As I sat in the chair across from her in the kitchen, the mood was solemn. "*Tengo algo que decirte.*" What could she possibly have to say to me? She had made a *mánda* to the Virgin of Guadalupe, promising she would make a pilgrimage to Mexico City with me if I would return home safely from military service. It hit like a bombshell. I was familiar with *mándas*. People made them to God, to a particular saint, or the Virgin, vows to make some kind of personal sacrifice, often pilgrimages to a religious site in Mexico, in return for answered prayers. Once the petition was answered, it had to be repaid, or run the risk of eternal damnation, I had heard.

"*Tienes que ir conmigo.*" "But why do I have to go?" I protested. "It was *you* who made the *mánda*, not me!" I was furious. I had no intention of disrupting my long-awaited freedom with this silly nonsense. She began to cry, then

123

in a tone of vehemence retorted, *"Sábes, a mi no me importa lo que tu pienses. Vas conmigo; es todo! Despues, te puedes ir al infierno, si quieres!"* The vehemence in her words stung me. I would go with *her,* that was it; and afterward, I could go straight to hell if I wanted. I stormed out of the room in a fury.

The next day, she set the date for our pilgrimage. We took a taxi to the Greyhound bus terminal downtown, and bought two tickets to Calexico. There, we would cross the border, pick up a train in Mexicali which would take us to Guadalajara, where another bus would take us to Mexico City, and the Basilica of Our Lady of Guadalupe.

On the way to Mexicali, we hardly spoke two complete sentences to each other. When we reached the border, we disembarked, and a taxi took us to the train station. It was late August and extremely hot and humid. We boarded the train, which was an hour and a half late, and settled into hard wooden seats in a sleeper car, our cramped home for the next three miserable days. "At least this heap has air conditioning," I thought to myself. But a couple of hours later, as the train chugged into the desert, the hiss of cold air squeezing through the air-conditioning vents went silent! A cauldron of heat consumed us. A few moments later, the conductor entered our car. "Something is temporarily wrong with the air conditioning," he said apologetically, "but don't worry, it will be fixed soon."

"Welcome to Mexico," I mumbled to myself sarcastically.

I forced open the window, but the heat from outside was far worse, so I slammed it shut again! I began to complain to my mother, who sat silently next to me. I blamed her for this. "This is your entire fault! I never wanted to want to come on this stupid trip in the first place!" And on the days that followed, I said terrible things to her, things I am too ashamed to write here.

By the time we reached Guadalajara, the temperature had cooled, and so had my temperament. Soon this whole ordeal would be over, and I would be released from any further obligations to anyone except myself. Here, the rail service ended, and we transferred to a bus for the day's trip to Mexico City. The scenery over the high mountains and into the Valley of Mexico was stunning.

The Basilica was like a huge, ancient mastodon, sinking to one side. I marveled at the serenity of the place. Despite my agnosticism, I knew this was *holy ground*. Peasants crammed the insides, and hordes of indigenous *peregrinos* could be seen approaching the entrance on their knees! I was humbled by their enormous faith. Inside, Mom went straight to the altar to give thanks to the Virgin for having answered her prayers. As I stood before the image of Guadalupe, housed in a fine gold-leafed frame high above the altar, a chill ran through me. I found a space in a pew and sat in silence.

The *mánda* paid for, we rented a room in a small hotel near the *Zocalo*, or Central Square. We agreed to stay a couple days, so we could see some of the sights. On the day before our scheduled return to Modesto, I said to her, "Mom, I have an old college friend, Jose Anguiano, who lives here, and I'm thinking of looking him up. I have his address. I'll take a taxi, and you wait for me in here in the hotel, OK? I won't be too long." She nodded.

The house was a slender, two-story building, with a small beauty salon, *Peinados Maria,* on the bottom floor. I vaguely remembered it from a visit years earlier with my college friends, Ray and Bob, when Jose still lived in Oakland, and his mother had given me some sweaters she had knitted, asking me to take them to him. I rang the bell, and his little sister Rosalia answered the door, and I introduced myself to her. "*Soy Ricardo, amigo de Jose en Los Estados Unidos.*"

"*Mamá! Mamá!*" she cried out. "*Es un amigo de Pepe!*" I was not accustomed to calling him Pepe. His mom greeted me with great fanfare. As I told her of our visit, and how we planned to leave the next day, she replied as if shocked, "*Mañana? No, no, se tienen que quedar!* Pepe is fine. He is married now and living in San Miguel de Allende. You must stay; bring your mother, so we can meet her! You have to see Pepe before you return!"

I was invited into the *sala,* and in single file, the rest of Pepe's five sisters marched in. The eldest, Elba, had blossomed into attractive young woman. Ranging from about ten to twenty years in age, they formally assembled themselves on the couch, the older ones sitting, the younger ones cuddled up on the floor, grinning and waiting for their brother's *gringo* friend to speak. But I was petrified to speak my broken Spanish, and they would giggle as I stumbled over words. I told them about all about Pepe, and when I was done, they chimed in unison, "Oh no, no.

You can't go back yet. There is so much to see in Mexico City, there's the Zócalo, Chapultepec Castle, the Museum of Anthropology, the pyramids at Teotihuacan! Bring your mother! We have to meet her!"

The next day, I brought my mother, and we were quickly convinced to stay in Mexico City, at least for a week, so the girls could show me around and the two mothers get to know each other. I loved being the center of attention; I mean, what guy wouldn't, with six lovely Mexican girls doting on him? Each day they toured me around Mexico City. Pepe's mother had found a room for us nearby, which we quickly rented.

One sister, Chela, stood out from the rest. She was petite, dark-skinned beauty with lovely hazel eyes. Our glances would lock, and, without consciously realizing it, we were being drawn to each other, as the pyramids, the mariachis at Garibaldi Square, and the floating gardens of Xochimilco plied their magic on us; before long, we were holding hands. The other sisters *saw*, nudging one another and giggling. It was all happening so quickly!

Soon the mothers *saw* too. *Graciela* was closely guarded. At seventeen, she was the apple of her mother's eye, and right hand in the beauty salon. Chela, as she was called, was shy and exuded a humility I seldom saw in the girls back home. To make a long story short, by midweek I found myself bringing flowers to her. Meanwhile, Pepe had been notified of our visit, and he and his wife arrived in Mexico City that Thursday. I told him about my feelings toward his little sister. "I think it's serious. What do you think if I were to ask her to marry me?"

"Well, Richard," he said, "I would be honored to have you as my brother-in-law, and if you want, I can put in a good word for you with my mother; but you know, Richard, I have only one concern about you and Chela. As you well know, you are a highly educated person, and so are all your friends. Chela is a simple girl with only a basic education. Are you sure she will fit into your world?"

"I'm not worried about that," I responded.

That night we decided to go to see the movie *My Fair Lady*, playing at a nearby movie theater off of Avenida Insurgentes, with Pepe and wife. Chela and I sneaked a couple of quick kisses during the film, our very first. We walked home hand in hand, me humming "On the

Street Where You Live" just loud so she could hear. Things were moving fast. Pepe, sensing that something was up, quickly excused himself and his wife with a simple *"Buenas noches,"* leaving us alone at the front door to the house. Then, after a long kiss, as if I had rehearsed it, I blurted out, "Chela, if I were to ask you to marry me, what would you say?" As far as I was concerned, it was not a marriage proposal per se, but only an hypothetical question. Her response was immediate and took me by surprise. "Sí," she said, and we sealed it with a long goodnight kiss.

That night as we returned to our room, I told my mother about my feelings toward Chela. "Mom, I have decided to marry Chela," and before I uttered another word, she looked skyward and began to cry with joy! I had never seen her like this before. *"Ay, gracias, Virgencita de Guadalupe! Gracias, Señora, por haberme concedido mis oraciones!"* They say God works in mysterious ways, and this trip, one that began as a disaster, had suddenly turned into a double miracle for my mom: the payment of the *mánda* and the probable marriage of her wayward son!

Pepe and his wife left for San Miguel the next day, as my mother and I formally *asked* for Chela's hand in marriage that Saturday. "I hope Pepe has put in a good word for me," I prayed silently. *"Pepe me ha dicho que el corresponde por ti, Ricardo,"* Doña Maria announced. He *had* come through and even vouched for me! My mother then told the parents about our intention to marry. It was Chela's mother who spoke. "Chela is too young, and she needs a little more time to mature. Go back to the United States, work for a year, save some money, and think about it, and if you still want to marry her, she will be here waiting for you." We were a bit let down, since Chela and I were probably both ready to get married the next day! We all shook hands, hugged, and uncorked a bottle of champagne for a toast and to formally seal the deal. Chela's father was sullen throughout.

The next day, a Sunday, my mom and I boarded a bus to Guadalajara, where we would pick up the train to Mexicali and then a bus back to Modesto. I felt ashamed of how I had treated her when this trip began. In the months that followed, Chela and I wrote dozens of grief-stricken love letters to one another and prayed for the months to pass. In ten months, when we could take it no longer, I returned to Mexico City to marry her. It was a simple but exquisite ceremony in a small, local cathedral and my brothers; Jesse and his wife, Dolores; and Eddie drove there in a brand-new Cadillac Ed had just bought, after hitting all five numbers in Reno with a five-spot at Keno. And so the bride arrived at the church in style.

Thou Shall Not Swear

"Thou shalt not swear neither
by heaven nor by earth, nor
by God, nor by anything, period."

She swore she would wear black
for the rest of her life when her son died.
A father swore he would never forgive
his daughter for bringing shame on the family:
*"Ya no eres mi hija! No quiero volver a verte!
Lárgate de mi casa!"*[1]

Maria swore she would go to church
every Sunday for the rest of her life
when her cow was spared. Don Aurelio
promised *La Virgen* he would make
a pilgrimage to Cathedral of Guadalupe
if *She* would just heal his son
beset by a mysterious sickness.

My mother vowed we would both
make a pilgrimage to Mexico City
to say thank you to *La Virgen de Guadalupe*
if She would bring me home safely from the Army.

A student once told me what happens when
one fails to *pay a manda.*[2] In her dead sister's
bedroom, doors open and shut by themselves;
things fly around in midair. It is her

spirit in search of someone to pay
the *manda* she was unable to before
she died. No one will; it is too heavy.

Note:

1. "You are no longer my daughter. I never want to see you again. Get out of of my house!"
2. a *manda* is a vow or promise made to God, the Virgin, or one of the many saints that "must bepaid" if a prayer is answered, at the risk of damnation

The Saint of Ansul Avenue

I *Return To Juarez*

How I came to live in the barrio one last time is a complicated story. After I married, I brought my wife back to the US with no real plans for our future, so we stayed with my mother while we got our bearings. Mom was delighted that her prodigal son had finally settled down and married a "good Mexican girl." She loved her new daughter-in-law, who she called "*muchacha*" (girl). It didn't take long for my wife to endear herself to her new mother, addressing her formally as "Señora Lupita."

But the lure of the Bay Area did not fade, so after a short time we moved to Oakland, found a nice little duplex on Harrison Street, and I was rehired at the flower shop I worked at during my stint in college. It was a short walk to the shop at Mayfair Shopping Center on Broadway, and we soon found part-time work for my wife there, too. A few months later, my old high school buddy, Bob Hamilton, who had just moved to Oakland, found an old two-story, house just off College Avenue that had an upstairs apartment for rent. We quickly fell in love with it and moved in.

Sometime later, while visiting my wife's family in Mexico City, we spoke to Pepe, who was still living in San Miguel de Allende, managing a hotel there, about the idea of going into business together with a small flower shop in town. San Miguel is a beautiful colonial town with fine churches, plazas, and cobblestone streets. With the host of American tourists there, it would be a lucrative venture, we agreed. But when we returned, and I told my mother about the idea, she was distraught. "There is no life in for you in Mexico," she lamented.

Regardless of her admonition, we left our apartment in Oakland to our good friends, Rick and Nancy Banker, and Chela and I moved to *San Miguel de Allende*. We found a small locale near the central plaza and quickly went into business. I would take a three-hour bus ride once a week to *La Merced*, a gigantic marketplace in Mexico City, to buy fresh flowers and supplies. But business at our shop was tepid and in less than a year, we discovered that my mother had been right: there was nothing in Mexico for us.

Again, we returned to Modesto, moved in with my mom, and I got a job with another florist in town while we decided on our next move. Not long after we married, my wife's nudging began.

"When are we going to have a baby?"

"Not now. Let's get to know each other first. Let's travel, have a good time. I'll let you know when I am ready." In the barrio, a woman married for a year with no baby was highly suspicious.

Three years had passed, and I worried about how much longer I could dodge her question. I had never imagined myself married and even less, being a father, but when the urge came, it came swiftly: "Let's have a baby! I'm ready now." Needless to say, my wife was ecstatic. I wanted the occasion to be something special. "We'll do it tomorrow night," we agreed. After work the next day, I made up a special bouquet of flowers and got a bottle of champagne. "What's the occasion?" my mother asked as I walked through the kitchen door. "Mom, we've decided to have a baby," I announced. *"Que bueno"*, she said sullenly, *"ya era tiempo."* And it was about time. *"Y eso para que es?"* she said, pointing in the direction of the champagne. "It's to celebrate with." And with a look of consternation she quipped, *"Ten cuidado, despues le va gustar y no la vas a poder sacar de las cantinas."* My wife and I looked at each other incredulously and laughed. I could not picture having to drag my alcoholic wife out of bars, just because of this innocent sip of champagne! That night we made love as never before, knowing that we were literally *sowing the seed* for our first child.

II *The House on Ansul Avenue*

Soon after, I began to look for an apartment we could move into which would have room for our new baby. It had never occurred to me to inquire about my uncles' house just down the street that had lain empty for years after their deaths. When I called my cousin Sally, who lived in Bakersfield, she told me she would "think about it." The old wooden house, probably built during the 1920s, had three small bedrooms, a modest kitchen and living room, a tiny bathroom, a washroom, and a basement with a door that opened from the kitchen floor. I remembered going down into the cellar as a kid and seeing all the fruits my aunt had canned arranged on wooden shelves. I loved the smell of wet dirt.

It was to this very house my mother sent me on many times when I was a kid and became *empachado,* or constipated. "This is what you get for eating green apricots. *Ándale, véte a ver a tu tia pa' que te sóbe.*" I dreaded this moment. My *Tia Juana* knew how to *sobar,* or massage. I would strip to my *chonies* and, tossing me onto her bed, she vigorously rubbed my arms, legs, and belly with smelly oils. It hurt! When she was done, she would grab a handful of skin from my back and stomach with both hands and actually pull me off the bed! I could hear the skin pop as it separated from the tissue underneath! Other times, she threw in an enema for good measure.

Like Flores Avenue, Ansul was an unlighted, pot-holed, dirt street without even a street sign on it. It was named after a chemical plant on the corner of Hosmer Street that made fire extinguishers. On windy days, the smell of sulfur permeated the barrio. But the best part of living here would be that we were only a few houses away from my mother's place, and my wife would have a companion during the day who could speak Spanish to her.

In front of the house, facing the street was a small cement porch, a lawn bordered by low hedges, and two orange trees. A cement sidewalk led to the front door, and the dirt driveway to a rickety old garage in the backyard. There was a shed where my *Tio* Quiríno kept his tools, with a small space where he stored his homemade wine.

A few days later my cousin called.

"Sure, you can have the house," she said.

"How much do you want for rent?"

"Is fifty dollars a month OK?" I tried not to sound too excited.

"Uh—sure, that would be fine." I sat in shock.

I could not believe we were going to have our first house, and for only fifty bucks a month! We moved in and quickly began to turn the empty house into a home by completely furnishing it from goods purchased at Goodwill, Salvation Army, and many of the secondhand stores on Crows Landing Road. All that was needed was a little love, sandpaper, paint, and my wife's creative touch to turn the secondhand items into conversation pieces. From the nearby brickyard, I confiscated bricks at night and used them to build shelves, stands, and cupboards. My mom was delighted to have us nearby, only a short walk from her house to ours.

After living there about a year, one day I reconnected with Bill Briggs. "Briggs" was a friend of Travis Ball, Phil Linhares's cousin, who I had both met at Roosevelt Junior High School. We met informally in Oakland a few years earlier, when I was going to college, and Travis was attending a trade school there. Briggs, who had just finished his military duty, was living alone in a small motel in downtown Modesto, and desperately looking for an apartment. I asked him if he would like to move in with us. We would go halfers on the rent, the food, and the utilities.

He leaped at the offer. We gave him the extra bedroom and he would become *Tio Bill* to our son Michaelangelo, who was born soon afterward. Briggs was a psych tech at the Modesto State Hospital, the *Bug House,* as he jokingly called it. He was smart, witty, well-read, and a huge fan of Hemingway and Steinbeck, like I was. He also loved drinking red wine, bullshitting, and listening to jazz, and quickly fell in love with my wife's cooking and hot salsa! He would join us as we shopped for the best bargains on groceries at the various stores and stands on Crows Landing Avenue. It turned out that Briggs and I were both caught up in the popular notion of the 1960s that to truly live, one had to *go back to nature,* just like the characters in a Steinbeck novel. And so, began our little *commune* on Ansul Avenue.

At first, the neighbors in the barrio were a little suspicious about our arrangement. They had a natural suspicion of *Americanos,* especially one living among them. But Briggs's easygoing and sincere manner quickly won them over, especially Doña Carmen, Charley and Raul's mom who lived next door, who, despite her atrocious English and Briggs' crude Spanish, became best buddies with him.

True to form, Briggs arrived one day with two baby chicks, one he named Chicken Chit, and the other Chicken Chet. In our backyard, he built a pen with two-by-fours and chicken wire, and when the hen started laying eggs, he would don a heavy coat and a cowboy hat for protection from Chicken Chet, who attacked anyone daring to enter the pen to gather them up. Soon after, when on a trip to the feed store for chicken feed, he saw a boxful of pups at the entrance and fell in love with one he brought home, naming him Carlitos. For a time the two were inseparable. After all, a *real man* had to have a dog at his side. Thus, when Carlitos disappeared one day, Briggs was devastated. After talking to a lady at the animal shelter who told him of a ring of people in Modesto who were abducting and selling dogs for lab experiments, Briggs went to Turner Hardware, purchased an axe handle, and, ready to bash in their heads, set out to track down people he had learned dealt in the illicit trade. Thank God he never found the ones who abducted Carlitos. "I'd probably be in prison now," he chuckles as we recall the story.

But besides sharing the cost of food and rent, and the camaraderie, Briggs and I shared a love for red wine, and we prided ourselves in finding the cheapest prices. One day, we stumbled across a wine called Vino Americano, a burgundy that a convenience store on Ninth Street sold for ninety-nine cents a gallon! And that was that. It became our liquor of choice for as long as we lived in that house. After dinner, we spent many fine evenings getting *smashed* and listening to records of Bill Evans, Coltrane, Miles Davis, and Dave Brubeck on the stereo. As our talk became more spirited, we drank more Vino Americano, and readied for the arrival of *T.S. Delgado.*

In an abrupt transition from the soft-spoken, mild-mannered person we all knew and loved, Briggs *became* T.S. Delgado, a drifter with a loud gruff voice who boasted of death, booze, and women. He was a worldly bum who rode the rails in search of adventure. My wife and I cracked up at this miscreant who regularly frequented our living room. Curiously, when Briggs was sober, he never spoke of T. S. Delgado. One day, years later, when Briggs stopped drinking, T. S. Delgado never again visited us.

During my wife's pregnancy, we painted and prepared the extra bedroom for our new baby. My brother Eddie was especially proud that we had delivered another Rios to carry on the family name. On the day my wife and son were released from the hospital, Ed picked them up in his Cadillac, and personally delivered them to the house on Ansul Avenue. *"Enseñenle a hablar Español!"* my mother chimed. And our son would grow up to speak Spanish; my wife and I saw to that. Mom visited us more now. Our back gate opened to the alley that divided the barrio and to the back gate of my mother's house. "Ya-Ya! Ya-Ya! Ya-ya!" he would scream, and rush to hug her around the knees. We never knew how the nickname for her began, but it stuck, and when our son Fernando was born three years later, their grandma would remain "Ya-Ya" to them. The Ansul house would leave us with great memories.

III. *Turning On, Tuning In, and Dropping Out*

My life should have been complete at this point. I had a college degree, had completed my military service, finally married, and had a son; yet, I had no idea what I was supposed to do with a master's degree in art, and making a living by selling my art was out of the question. Modesto held no real opportunities for me. I continued to fantasize of returning to the Bay Area, but for now life in the barrio would do. Maybe I could teach art?

I began to apply for a teaching position at various colleges, including my alma mater in Oakland. "Dear Mr. Rios, despite your impressive qualifications, we have no positions open at this time. Thank you for your consideration." I was to memorize the response. It became obvious to me that no one was going to hire me without teaching experience, or without an extensive résumé of museum or gallery exhibitions of my work. I became cynical. What the hell had six hard years of a college education gotten me? So I resolved to "turn on, tune in, and drop out." In way, I had come *full circle.* I had started in the barrio, and here I was again. If nobody had use for my talent, to hell with them!

However, with a gnawing ounce of optimism, a belief that God had some kind of plan for me, I enrolled in a credential program at the state university in nearby Turlock. I'd never planned on becoming a teacher, though I'd successfully served a year as a teaching assistant at in college, alongside my mentor, master teacher Ralph Borge, and I loved it. I knew I could handle myself with college students, but now I even considered the possibility of teaching in elementary, junior high, or high school. But I soon felt out of place in the program among the smug *white* kids, fresh out of college, who seemed to sap up all the teachers' attention. For one course, we were required to make individual class presentations, so I put together an ambitious multi-media project using my own drawings, poems, and slides. It bombed. But my ambitious stint in the credential program ended abruptly one day, after spending days creating a series of lesson plans for an imaginary high school art class. I carefully designed each lesson to teach the student to see not only the beauty in nature, but also the subtle relationships between nature and art, incorporating lessons in watercolor painting, charcoal drawing and design, and closely following my instructor's guidelines.

When I entered the office, the Ivy League clad instructor greeted me, and I took a seat next to him. Against the walls and on the floor were stacks of papers and student projects. Sure he would be impressed, I handed him my lesson plans. Holding the packet in the palm of his left hand, with his right hand he quickly thumbed through each page, pausing now and then to read. Evidently he was a rapid reader, because in two minutes he had leafed through my entire project. "I'm sorry, Mr. Rios, but this will never work in a classroom environment. You don't seem to understand—"

I turned crimson and stood up. "But I *do* understand. I understand clearly that I can never fit into *your* preconceived notion of what art is. I put a lot of work into this assignment," I complained. "And you just thumbed through it without even reading it!"

Who did this *greenhorn* think he was, fresh out of college, telling *me* my lesson plans "would never work?" Me, who had stood in front of Da Vinci's *"Mona Lisa"*, Picasso's *"Guernica"*, and Goya's *"Disasters of War"* in the Louvre, and underneath Michelangelo's Sistine Chapel in the Vatican! I had seen the works of Rembrandt and Vermeer in the Rijkes Museum in Amsterdam, for God's sake! As he stumbled for words to defend his evaluation of my project, I grabbed it from him, stormed out of his office, and never returned to the program.

Still determined to find something on the positive side, I began to list the benefits of my situation. Life in the barrio was uncomplicated: no smog, no commuter traffic, and no artsy-fartsy pseudo-intellectuals to put up with. I was ready for the simplicity of the Central Valley, long hot summers, and the sweet smell of fruit orchards and stewed tomatoes from the cannery. This was *real*. Just maybe this was where I belonged.

Ironically, it would turn out to be one of the most creative periods in my life. I painted. I worked on large charcoal drawings on butcher paper, and I built *found object* sculptures in our yard. We bought a 1954 Chevy station wagon, and I would drive along Crows Landing Road, stopping at the various secondhand stores and junk yards and buy old wooden chairs, boxes, frames, dolls, wire, and ceramic vases, offering the owners ten dollars to fill up the back of the station wagon. Hours would be spent in our back yard nailing, gluing, sawing, and wiring together a conglomeration of disparate objects into my "sculptures" that I nailed to the garage, in trees, or on the tops of fence posts lining the driveway. The neighbors must have thought I had gone nuts, but I loved watching them stop to study each piece, scratching their heads in wonder. Our yard became a virtual barrio art gallery.

When our son Michaelangelo was born in 1969, and I finally became a father, I fully embraced it. I loved being a dad and making things for him. One day, I cut a three-foot branch from a tree, stripped off the bark, notched the ends, and fashioned it into a jumper for him. With strips of leather I found in a dumpster in town, I wove a cradle he could sit into, hanging the entire contraption from the doorpost leading from the kitchen into the living room, with a large spring. He would spend hours bouncing up and down on it.

Another time, I made him a wooden race car from plywood, two-by-fours, and cast-off tricycle wheels. I even designed a steering wheel for it with ropes leading to the front axles, which I had bolted on in a way that allowed it to be turned right or left! I loved wheeling him down Ansul Avenue. But my masterpiece was a swing I made for him, a single-seater, double-winged WWI-style airplane, which I painted orange and decorated with British insignias on the sides and on the wings. I hung it from a large branch of one of the orange trees in the front yard, and Michaelangelo was the envy of the neighborhood. He loved to sit inside it while his dad pushed him back and forth.

I would also try my hand at farming at the Ansul house, planting *chiles*, corn, tomatoes, and even a few cannabis plants, though I was very paranoid about that. One Sunday morning, my wife and I were awakened by a knock on the front door. We were still in bed, so I got up to answer it. Through the front window, I saw some kind of officer standing there. He wore a greenish-colored uniform with an official-looking patch on his shoulder. I slowly cracked open the door. "Yes, can I help you?"

"Good morning, I am from the Agriculture Department, and we are doing searches of neighborhoods for a pest that has been invading plants. Can you give us permission to search your yard?" I froze. I stuttered. "Uh, um, can you wait a minute while I get dressed?" I raced to the bedroom and dragged my wife out of bed. "Quick, get up; it's some guy from the Agriculture Department, and he wants to look at plants in our yard! You go to the door and keep him busy in the front yard, while I cover up the marijuana plants in the back!" All I could think of as I frantically searched for something to cover the two plants with was, "Oh, *shit*. This is it. I'm gonna get life in prison, or the death penalty, for this." Remember, this was the 1960s, and some poor guy had just been given life in prison for a matchbox full of weed!

In broken English, Chela kept the guy busy in the front yard, pausing to point out every rosebush on the sides of the driveway leading to the back yard. She was charming, and men were quickly attracted to her. When they joined me in the backyard, I had already covered the two marijuana plants with some corrugated tin panels I had found behind the shed. I continued to distract him. "Yeah, I'm trying my hand at growing tomato plants, but they seem a little small, don't you think? Should I put fertilizer on them?" Satisfied, the guy thanked us and left. I knew someone had turned us in, but we never found out who it was. The next day, I pulled out the two plants.

In time, the Ansul house became a small cultural and intellectual oasis. Friends from the Bay Area visited with news of the outside world, and they ate good Mexican food, drank beer, sipped tequila and cheap wine, smoked *weed,* and seemed to envy our little world. Sometimes, they left me little tokens of weed, hashish, or mescaline, though I was cautious of taking anything stronger than marijuana. The old-timers in the barrio often warned of how you could go insane by smoking marijuana! For me, beer, wine, and occasional shots of tequila were enough, so when a young friend of Bob Hamilton urged me to take LSD with him, I refused. "Dude, you gotta try it, man; it's *far out man,* you know? I'll leave you some, and you can take it whenever you feel like it." Though I accepted it, I had no intention of ever using it.

But one day, months later, I finally decided to take the miniscule flake of LSD I had been saving for a special occasion. Though I had heard of people hallucinating or having *bum trips* on *acid,* I went ahead; on the contrary, it turned out to be quite a *good trip*, but a cautionary one. I would take it early in the morning and that way have the whole day to experience it. My wife largely ignored me that day, leaving me to my own devices.

As I let the tiny flake, which looked like a piece of dandruff stuck on a piece of scotch tape, dissolve on my tongue, an incredible euphoria slowly consumed me. It was sweet-tasting. The blue of sky intensified, the greens of plants became vivid, and I felt a powerful sense of oneness with all living things.

As the high intensified, I decided to go for a walk along the railroad tracks toward the Tuolumne River. I became totally absorbed with the unique shape and color of every stone scattered along the rails. I began to stuff my pockets with the uniquely shaped ones. I gathered up pieces of bones, nails, and discarded wine bottles, making several trips to our backyard to deposit them, and returned for more. Something was driving me forward. Soon, I found myself cutting branches of various sizes and lengths from trees and also lugging them back to the yard. When I had finished, I looked at the pile and instantly knew I was going to make a mobile. I began by inserting a large eye screw into the crossbeam of the entrance to the garage and tying a large curved branch to it with fishing line. It would support the weight of the smaller branches tied to it in descending order, longest to the shortest. From each of these, I strung stones of various shapes, colors, and sizes, along with bottles, nails, and bolts, all the while finding the perfect balancing point for each one. Without realizing, I had spent the entire day making it.

Done, I was extremely proud of my accomplishment, calling my wife out to see it. *"Muy bonito,"* she said and walked back inside the house. It was late afternoon, and I still felt high, so I went into the house, filled a glass with white wine, and walked out into our front yard, settling into a lawn chair. The drone of passing airplanes mesmerized me. I felt close to God, to space, and to the living universe. I became mesmerized watching a monarch butterfly that had wandered into the yard. As it meandered from flower to flower, I realized I had never seen an object of such exquisite beauty. Suddenly, it hovered just above my head, and parked itself squarely on my nose! The prickly legs tickled, and I froze, fearing I might frighten it off. But it just remained there! I was afraid to even breathe. I wanted to call my wife so she could share the moment with me, but I feared that might scare off the butterfly. When it finally flitted away a few moments later, I felt as if I had been the recipient of a gift from God, a confirmation that I mattered—that if I was patient, something great awaited me.

But by early evening there was no evidence that I was coming down from the intense high. In truth, I was tired and just wanted it to end. It had been more than eight hours, so I went into our bedroom and lay on the bed. I became afraid. "How long does this *shit* last?" I thought to myself. "What if it doesn't end?" I was suddenly gripped by a powerful paranoia. By ten o'clock, the effects of my acid trip had finally worn off, and I fell off into a deep sleep. That night I had a dream; or was it a vision? I saw my deceased uncle, Quirino, walking up the driveway toward me. He was wearing khaki pants and a work shirt. My *tio* was short, stocky and unobtrusive, a man of few words. He worked mostly at farm labor, made wine, and loved working in his yard; it had been about three years since he and my *tia* Juana had passed away.

I was torn between terror and joy, but the broad smile on his face reassured me. Looking at the house and the rosebushes on each side of the driveway, he nodded in approval and said, "Thank you for taking such good care of my house." That was the first and last time I would ever take acid.

But I also experienced *natural highs* at the Ansul house. I began to read books on spirituality and the occult. I became enthralled with Zen Buddhism and ideas of reincarnation and karma. On Sunday mornings, I looked forward to lectures by spiritual guru Alan Watts on the relationship between Christianity and Zen Buddhism that aired on a radio station from the Bay Area. I devoured books by famous psychic Edgar Cayce, and more books about life after death, dreams, and dream interpretation. I even bought a deck of tarot cards and pompously did experimental *readings* for my friends. How I must have bored them with babble about the world of mind and spirit! I had long ago given up on going to Mass, and would have probably been excommunicated, had the church known of my mystical delvings. I remembered sermons condemning the use of Ouija boards as satanic, but they intrigued me.

It was also at the Ansul house that I first tried my hand at making wine, though I had no idea how to make it. "It can't be that hard," I convinced myself. Next to the house was an abandoned field of Thompson grapes. In my uncle's shed, I found a large metal tub that I used to crush the grapes in, and used netting to cover the juice with. I removed my shoes and socks, rolled up my pants, hosed off my feet, and stepped inside, just as I had seen done in movies and European paintings. The hot grape juice squirting between my toes was sensual. One day, as I was crushing grapes, my mother stopped by to visit. *"Muchacho, cochino!"* she cringed and said.

"How can you drink that stuff after crushing it with your dirty feet?"

"But Mom, I hosed off my feet, and besides, I'm *your son*, your own flesh and blood! You mean to tell me you won't drink wine crushed by your son's own feet?"

"No, no I wouldn't!" I pretended to be hurt, laughing at her naïveté. I'd never told anyone about the problems I'd had with athlete's foot, growing up.

But Doña Carmen was not so picky. During the fermentation process, she would visit daily, pretending to be neighborly.

"Como viene el vino, Ricardo?"

"Muy bien, Señora Carmen, quiere una provadita?"

And we would saunter into the garage for a "little taste" of the new wine from a plastic coffee cup I had hanging on a nail.

One day, probably sensing that our time at the Ansul house was ending, Briggs put his arm around my shoulder and said thoughtfully, "You know, Richard, you're the Saint of Ansul Avenue." I was obviously flattered but simultaneously taken aback at the irreverent comparison.

"Me, a saint? Come on, Briggs."

"No, no. I mean it. You are a saint." But being the shameless sinner I was, I couldn't accept the title in good conscience. It felt almost sacrilegious. Maybe if we stretched it a little, the moniker might work. But to me, a saint was a person who denied self, a martyr willing to die for his beliefs, and most certainly not one who smoked pot and drank Vino Americano!

IV *A Farewell to Juarez*

But the years we lived at the Ansul house would turn out to be my last in Juarez. We would buy our first house on Acacia Street a couple of miles further south from the barrio, where our second son Fernando was born. Briggs would continue to live with us, and in time went on to get his own college degrees. In 1972, while working at Hart Floral downtown, I received a phone call from Chris Martinez, chair of the Chicano Studies Department, at San Joaquin Delta College in Stockton. "Is this *the* Richard Rios?" "Yes?" I hesitated. "You come *highly* recommended by a couple of your buddies in Sacramento, Jose Montoya and Esteban Villa. How would you like to teach a course for us in Chicano literature?" Villa and Montoya were old college buddies who had also graduated from art school, gone on to become art teachers, and formed the RCAF, *Royal Chicano Air Force*, a coalition of Chicano artists in Sacramento. "What's *Chicano literature?*" I asked. "Don't worry about it. I am sending you some books. Read them." I quickly applied for the position, and I was hired! That summer I plowed through a stack of novels by Chicano authors. I had no idea there was such a thing. But as I read these authors, I realized I had lived many of the things they wrote about. I finished the last book just in time for my first class in September. And I was ready. I would no longer be a dropout.

When I walked into my first three-hour Monday-night class, it was packed from wall to wall with anxious brown faces, with more students lined up in the hallway outside the door, waiting to get in! Trembling,

I timidly began my lecture, carefully following the extensive notes I had prepared. But by the break, and hour and half later, I had completely exhausted my notes! After break, I began to tell them some of the stories that would one day make up the heart of this book. My experiences growing up in Juarez would serve me well. For the first four years, I would commute the sixty miles round-trip from Modesto to Stockton, but in 1976, my wife and two sons would move there permanently. Thirty-three years later, I would retire from teaching.

Un Dia a la Vez, Dios Mio

"*Aqui me quiero morir*," my mother would continue to remind us for several years after my wife and I left Modesto and permanently moved to Stockton. "I want to die *here*, in *my* home," she begged after she was diagnosed with cervical cancer in the late 1970s, and it became harder for her to care for herself, despite the fact that my wife regularly drove the sixty-mile round-trip to Modesto to take her to the bank, or the doctor, or shopping. After our repeatedly asking her to sell her house and move to move in with us, she finally conceded to move in with my sister Shirley, who had a small space over an outbuilding we converted into a living space. Left with few options, she was forced to sell the house on Flores St. and leave the old barrio that had been her home and that of her children for so many years.

One day, years earlier, Mom had asked me to listen to a song on an eight-track cassette called "*Un Dia a La Vez*" (One Day at a Time), by *Los Tigres del Norte*. She wanted me to learn it and sing it to her on the guitar. "*Quiero que la aprendas y que me la cantes con tu guitarra,*" she said. As I listened to it, she handed me a piece of paper with part of the song's lyrics already scribbled in pencil on it. The singer asked God to help him learn to live "one day at a time." Sensing that her own mortality was near, the song seemed to have a special meaning for her. "Sure, Mom," I promised, "I'll learn it." But in time, like so many other promises I had made to her, I forgot all about it and so had she, I thought.

The tiny apartment in East Stockton made it so much easier to care for her, since we lived across town, and my wife and sister could more easily tend to her needs. My wife and I helped to paint the rooms, and my brother-in-law, Abe, portioned the space into a small living room and kitchenette, a bedroom, and a bathroom, with a shower and toilet. He put in electrical outlets and connected gas lines for a stove and a heater. We found a used hospital bed in a medical supply store, making it easier for her to get in and out of than a regular bed. Our Sunday ritual was to attend Mass and visit her afterward. We all looked forward to a breakfast of fried eggs, refried beans, and her homemade flour tortillas. Our sons, Michaelangelo and Fernando, loved these visits with their *Ya-Ya*. Though she put up a good front with smiles and a good sense of humor, the increasing pain was plainly visible on her face.

One Sunday, after breakfast, I again saw the eight-track tape, sitting on a small table near her stereo. As I fondled it in my hands, I flood of shame engulfed me. Here it was two years later, my mom dying of cancer, and I had yet to learn the song I had promised to sing for her! I shoved the tape into the player, replaying it over and over until I had copied down all the lyrics.

In the weeks that followed, I quickly learned it. It fit nicely into an easy three-chord pattern. Because I wanted it to be special for Mom, I invited my *compadre,* Flavio Gonzalez, who played *requinto* (melody) on guitar, and my good friend Domingo Reyes, who had a beautiful, booming voice, to our house to rehearse the song. When we had arranged it in three-part harmony, the three of us, along with my wife, drove to her tiny apartment and, without letting on, tiptoed up the flight of wooden stairs, into her bedroom, and walked in singing *"Un Dia a La Vez"* to her, surrounding her bed; my own voice broke several times during the song, as I fought back the tears. She tearfully thanked us, and I felt complete, knowing how happy I had made her, if only for this moment. I owed it to her.

A couple of months later, in late 1984, she was admitted to the hospital. As she pathetically studied the blinking monitors and freeways of intravenous tubes, and listened to the beeps of monitors connected to her, she looked at me in desperation saying, *"Cuando se llegue mi tiempo, no me tengan con todos esos tubos. Dejen me ir."* I promised that when her time came, we would not keep her connected to "all those tubes", or life support, and *let her go* in peace. During one of her last days at the hospital, she was in and out of consciousness, and for longer periods of time. Though I was not particularly prayerful, I asked God to bring her suffering to an end.

But to the end, she never lost that caustic sense of humor that was hers alone, which I think I inherited from her. One day, as she dozed off for longer than usual, I wondered if this might be the end. Suddenly, she jerked up from her pillow, and with her eyes wide open, stared around the room in a stupor. When she finally recognized me, she laughed and said, "*Híjole, ya me andaba llevándo La Pelóna!*" I couldn't help but laugh at the outrageous image of *Old Baldy*, what Mexicans playfully refer to as the Grim Reaper, carting off with my mother! I reached for her hand, and she quickly took mine, and I was stunned by the realization that before this moment, we had never held hands! She turned to my wife on the other side of the bed, taking her hand too.

"*Cuidame mucho a mi muchacho,*" she begged her, "*cuidame mucho a mi muchacho.*"

"*Si, Señora Lupita, yo se lo cuido, no se preocupe,*" my wife promised. She would take good care of *her boy*. Mom's death was uneventful. A few days later, she was moved to a nearby convalescent home. My brothers and sisters were in and out of the room, and one day my brother Eddie approached me in the waiting room and said sullenly, "Everyone agrees that it should be you, Richard, to tell the doctor to remove her from life support."

"Me? Why me?" I protested. "I think John should do it, he's the oldest!"

I had imagined it would be an easy thing to honor Mom's request, but it wasn't. The finality and awesome weight of the act crushed me, as I instructed the doctor to remove the tubes.

"She's not in pain," he assured me. "She will go slowly as her body shuts down."

I wanted to be by her side to witness her final breath. My wife and I spent hours at her bedside, but the tiny wisp of life inside her did not go willingly. We were all exhausted. On the last day, I convinced my wife we should go home for a few hours to rest, but before leaving, I leaned close to Mom's ear.

"Mom, we're a little tired and going home to rest. We'll be back in a couple of hours, OK?" Unconscious, she gave no indication she had heard me.

"She will not die unless we are here," I promised my wife. "I know," she replied.

When we returned later that day, Mom was still breathing, but barely. I watched a tiny vein in her neck pulsate with longer intervals in between, until it finally stopped, and I remembered the words of her lifelong prayer to God: "*Lo que le pido a Dios, es que no déje que ningúnos de mis hijos se muéran antes de mi.*" In His great benevolence, God had answered her prayer that her none of children die before her, something she would not have been able to bear.

"*No hay amor como el amor de una madre.*" And I came to understand, at last, her belief that no greater love exists than a mother's love for her children.

We buried her in a rural cemetery a few miles from a small community called French Camp, tucked between Stockton and Modesto, a place she said had an air of peace and tranquility about it. "*Mira,*" she said one day as we drove past it, "*ahi quiero que me entierrén. Me paréce un lugar muy tranquílo.*" My wife and I saw to it that the words *Un Dia a La Vez, Dios Mio* be inscribed on her headstone.

Mother's Day

It was Mother's Day, several years after Mom died, that my wife and I decided to take some flowers to her grave after Sunday mass. We had not visited for a while, and the site was unkempt, with a solitary bouquet of flowers my sister Shirley had probably brought earlier that day. We were there alone, odd for a Mother's Day, except for a couple of noisy crows circling overhead. A farm labor camp nearby pulsated with life: the screams of children playing while the women pinned laundry on clotheslines and men buried their heads under open hoods of cars.

We tidied up the the gravesite, and I arranged the bouquet I had brought into a vase. As we sat on an adjacent tombstone in silence, my mind drifted back to the Mother's Days of old, when the whole family, my brothers and sisters, nephews, nieces, and grandkids all congregated to Mom's house—Mom, the matriarch whose tiny house barely held the throngs of family on that day of days. Little did we all know it would not always be that way.

Mother's Day at our house actually began days earlier, with Mom preparing the ingredients she would use for the array of dishes, especially the *enchiladas* she made for brother Eddie (we all knew it). Tortillas had to be made, red chili sauces simmered, onions diced, and lettuce shredded. Beans had to be cooked, then refried. *Sopa de Arroz* (Spanish rice) was readied. Meanwhile, she prepared the special breakfast for my brother Jess, who was always first to arrive, about nine in the morning: scrambled eggs fried into her hot chile sauce alongside two fried eggs, refried beans, and fresh, handmade flour tortillas.

Sister Shirley was next to arrive, bringing more dishes and quickly jumping in to help Mom cook. I always looked forward to the pork buns she was sure to bring. Next to arrive was brother Ed, Mom's *favorite,* though she insisted she loved us all "equally." I suppose he was my favorite too. He brought the champagne, which he dutifully loaded into the refrigerator. Then, he would head straight for the *enchiladas* that we all knew Mom had *really* made for him. Ed was the hugger and the kisser of the family (the rest of us weren't much for that kind of stuff), and, after hugging and kissing Mom first, he proceeded to do the same to the rest of us. Once, he even kissed me smack on the lips, taking me completely by surprise! Then he would sit down for the feast. His wife, Joyce, brought the best lemon merangue pies, made with fresh lemons picked from trees in their backyard. However, after eating all that food, I never had room for a slice, and when I was ready later in the day, only crumbs remained.

By now it was 11 o'clock and my brother John would be next to arrive in an old Mercury clunker, which he liked to brag, had over 150,000 miles on it. He was the oldest, the quiet one. He usually came alone. Since I was the youngest, and my older brothers often had little time for me, John did, always genuinely interested to know how I was and how I was doing in school.

Last to show was my sister Mary and my crazy brother-in-law, Elias. By now it was one o'clock, and most everybody had eaten. My brother-in-law loved his liquor, and I would sneak a few drinks with him when Mom wasn't looking. By the end of the day, he had always had a little too much to drink, and a couple of us would have to escort him to his car; all the while, Mary would profusely apologize to us.

Yet the highlight of the day began about two o'clock, after everyone had eaten, when I and my brothers Jess and Ed would take out their guitars and sing, with everyone jumping in. As far as I knew, there was no other family in our barrio that sang together and played guitars like ours did! They would start with romantic boleros, like "*Sin Ti*" and "*Solaménte Una Vez*", and as the day and drinks wore on, proceed to the hardcore *rancheras* and *corridos*, good old Mexican drinking songs like "*Ella*", "*El Hijo Desobediénte*", "*Valentín de La Sierra*", and "*Rosita Alvírez*"; songs about unrequited love, lust, passion, betrayal, and tragedy. Ed and Jess had the best voices of the family and carried fine, two-part harmonies. I loved singing with them, adding a third harmony whenever I could, and even though Mom always said "I can't sing," she sometimes surprised us with a muffled fourth harmony. These were the songs of *la gente,* the common people, from the heyday of popular Mexican music, the 30s, 40s and 50s; ballads from the Mexican Revolution. We would sing them, one after another, until dusk.

About midway through the songfest, Ed would uncork the champagne, and, once everyone was served, he would toast to Mom: "To the best mom in the world!" And we would would tip our glasses to her. She didn't like the taste of champagne, and, after much protest, she would tip her perfunctory glass along with her family, complaining all the while, "If I get tipsy, you'll all be to blame for it!" Glasses were filled again and again and the songs continued. "Sing *Ella!*" sister Mary would cry. "We already sang that one," I would remind her.

"So? Sing it again!"

Suddenly, someone would slip "*Zorba The Greek*", on the record player and Mary would be transformed! Snapping her fingers, and sensually gyrating from side-to-side, she *became* Anthony Quinn, on that deserted beach in Greece, as she danced the tune with inspired gusto for the boisterous crowd in that living room.

By now, verses were being repeated, songs halted in mid-verse, or fizzled out, as we forgot their lyrics and the liquor began to take its toll.

But no matter, the audience was insatiable and demanded more. "Hey, do you guys remember *Las Golondrinas?*" someone else would ask as we continued our round trips to the kitchen for refills of beer and champagne. And Mom, the queen, sat there among her subjects, proud, bursting with love for each of us. Then, at the end of the day, came the moment Mom knew would come, and dreaded, as we would beg, "Come on, Mama, sing a song, come on!" "Don't make me sing, please," she pleaded, "you know I can't sing…." I could always convince her by promising I would sing along with her. Cornered, and realizing she had no choice, I would start the song, then her tremulous, but melodic soprano voice joined mine to her favorite songs: "*A la Orilla de un Palmar*",

"*Cancion Mixteca*", and "*Rayando el Sol.*" After each song, we all clapped loudly, and she feigned embarrassment.

About six o'clock, those who lived furthest away would begin to drift out, each one carrying paper plates filled with leftovers. Mom and my sisters would begin the cleanup, washing dishes and carrying out bags of trash as the last of my brothers and sisters packed up their families and said their good-byes. John was always the last to leave, but before he left, he would ask Mom for a cup of coffee, and he and I would sit in the empty living room and talk, the eldest and the youngest, in mutual respect. At that was it. Another Mother's Day had passed.

At Mom's grave that Sunday, we recalled those bygone Mother's Days with a renewed fondness. Before we left, we stood, and the two of us spontaneously began singing out loud her song, "*Un Dia a La Vez*". Done, we prayed an Our Father, turned, and headed for the car. Mother's Day will never be the same as my brother Eddie passed away a few years ago, and I now see my aging brothers and sisters once a year, if I'm lucky.

The Last Train to Juarez

I t is a beautiful, sunny, summer morning, and I'm sitting in a train, my body rhythmically rocking back and forth to the clacking of the wheels. The wooden seat is hard. But what train is this? Where is it going? I am sitting on the left side of the car, and I suddenly realize I am on the Tidewater Southern heading toward downtown Modesto! But wait, this isn't even a passenger train; it never has been!

But it has seats. I look around, but there's no one else on board. The window is wide open. There's the old, two-story mansion we used to call the haunted house. I smell sulfur. Up ahead I see the old Ansul chemical plant, and I realize the train is heading into the heart of Juarez, my old barrio! But it's the present? Besides, I'm an adult now. What am I doing here? How did I get here? Then it hits me. Somehow, I've been transported back into time, and I'm being given the chance to see Juarez one last time, exactly the way it was when I was a kid!

But I have to stop trying to figure it out. The train is moving forward, and there is no time to waste. I lean out of the window as far as I can. I want to soak it all in. I'll ask questions later. I look down Hosmer Street as we slowly pass. I see the Hernandezes. Further down, my buddy Robert is standing in the middle of the street with a football in his hand. Behind him are the Casillas, and behind them, Ernie and Esther, Robert's brother and sister-in law. Now we are passing the dirt alleyway dividing the barrio. There's Petra, the *bruja*, who used to yell and babble to herself alone in her house, tending her pigeons. There's Tacho and his wife, and Doña Luisa and her husband, Timotéo, and at their side, Whitey, the dog from hell. He's barking at me!

I need to act quickly; there are people on both sides of the tracks lined up to watch the train pass! Doña Margarita, my mom's *comadre,* is on the side of her house, poking around at her plants of cilantro and *chiles.* Behind her, I see my mother! She's raking her backyard and sprinkling it with a water hose.

I rush to the window on the right side of the train! Just in time. And I wave at my *tios,* Quirino and Juana, who look sadly on. They are not waving. But that's the way they are. Further on the right, I see Charlie; Raul; Jesse, his older brother; and their mom and dad, Sabás and Carmen, in their backyard. But the train just keeps moving forward. I want to stop it, but I can't!

As we pass my street, Flores Avenue, I realize this is it. A cocktail of emotions engulfs me. I want to absorb every person, every smell, sight, and sound. I see my brothers and sisters standing in front of our house: John, Eddie, Jesse, Shirley, and Mary. And there am I with my dog, Skippy, grinning from ear to ear, his tail wagging wildly! I'm wearing my *pechéras,* painter's bib pants and my favorite boots. The people begin to dissolve, one by one, as I strain to look back, and this unstoppable machine plows forth, into the present.

I'm looking back at Juarez, now. If I lean out of the window any further, I'll fall out. We are passing the orchard in front of our house. The brick factory replaces the orchard, then River Road. There are tears in my eyes as the train begins to cross the bridge over the Tuolumne River, toward downtown Modesto, and my old barrio is no more.

I wake with a start! I'm in my own bed in Stockton, or is it Oakland? It's 8:19 in the morning. 1975! I'm flooded with an overwhelming feeling of joy and sadness, as I realize I've just ridden on the last train to Juarez. I chuckle aloud as I'm reminded of the old Zen story about a man who awoke from a dream not knowing if he was a man who dreamed he was a butterfly, or a butterfly who dreamed he was a man. From that moment on, I chose to be a butterfly who dreamed he was a man.